How to Get RICH
Selling Cars and Trucks
to Women!

ADVANCE PRAISE...

"I have seen Rebecca transform audiences of automotive sales and service professionals in her interactive seminars. This book is for anyone in our industry willing to learn the competencies needed to harness the economic power of the women's market. They're in the driver's seat now."

John Pockrus
Area Executive
Audi of America

"WOW! I've been in the car business for over 20 years, and I've never read a book so knowledgeable on selling to women. It has already increased our sales. Everyone that works for me will get a copy of this book!"

Brad Johnson
General Manger
Byers Dublin Chevrolet

"I have spent most of my 32-year career targeting women auto buyers and now, thanks to Rebecca and Marti, I have a play-book!"

Gabe Staino
Dealer Principle
Galloway Chrysler, Dodge

"Don't let the title mislead you. This is a book all automotive sales consultants should read. True professionals, male or female, can profit from a better understanding of what makes us all tick. It's a very enjoyable reading experience!"

Tom Carpenter
President
Saturn of Columbus

"This book has made such a profound impact on my approach to this business. For every opportunity you have to interact with a woman customer, this book gives you the tools to respond in the most effective way. I've witnessed first hand that if you listen for what her real needs are, and react accordingly, it really does build her trust, which translates into building the business, big."

Don Andres
Fixed Operations Director
Ricart Automotive

"The thing I like most about this book is being able to implement so many of the suggestions on day one. It has really made a measurable difference. We do a better job in sales and service with our women customers and prospects and this is directly attributable to what we've learned from Maddox Smye."

Kevin Parker
Executive Manager
Garber Management Group

"The Maddox Smye message is right on target. We all want to be treated with dignity and respect, and appreciated for who we are. This certainly carries over to our buying relationships. These folks provide a simple message with a powerful outcome for success. Everyone in the retail business should have this book on their 'must read' list."

Patricia Roberts
Director, Women's Retail Initiative
General Motors

How to Get RICH
Selling Cars
and Trucks
to Women!

REBECCA MADDOX, MBA, CPA

MARTI SMYE, PhD

Maddox Smye LLC
Naples, Florida

maddoxsmye
wiser about women

Published by:
Maddox Smye LLC
300 Fifth Avenue South, Suite 101
Naples, Florida 34102
www.maddoxsmye.com

Literary Agent:
Albert Zuckerman
Writers House
21 West 26th Street
New York, New York 10010

ISBN 0-9727637-4-0

PRINTED IN THE UNITED STATES OF AMERICA
10 9 8 7 6 5 4 3 2 1

CONTENTS

ACKNOWLEDGMENTS

From Rebecca...

Here's a confession…I never wanted to be a salesperson—ever. Growing up in Ohio, daughter of Dan Maddox, a Nabisco sales-man, I didn't think being in sales was a "real" profession. In my kid-view of the world, if you weren't a doctor, a lawyer, or a banker, you didn't have a real job. Almost any other career seemed infinitely more important than sales.

Time, age and wisdom change many things—including per-ception.

Fortunately, in my view and in public opinion, the sales profes-sion is gaining the respect it so seriously deserves. All successful people are in sales—first and most important, selling themselves. You simply can't "win" in life if you don't know the basics of sell-ing. In sales, you make things happen. You serve other people— saving them time and money and meeting their needs and desires—through the services and products you offer. I salute the dynamic men and women who have distinguished themselves as leaders in a field that transcends every other profession.

So here I am in sales, like my Dad. I've spent most of my life in corporate America selling in one form or another. Now, as an entrepreneur and business owner, I use my sales ability daily to persuade people to believe in me and the products and services of Maddox Smye. Thanks, Dad, for pursuing a sales vocation and demonstrating daily that serving other people is truly the highest calling. You've been the greatest role model and teacher. I only hope someday I can be as good you!

From Marti...

I too grew up in Ohio. Salineville, Ohio (population 1,397) is a little town that obviously had something good in the water, because in small towns, people understand that relationships count. The time spent on the front porch getting to know someone pays big dividends, not only for the initial sale, but for life. There are many lessons: loyalty comes from trust; trust comes from good listening; good listening comes from genuine caring.

And here's a tip for sales managers: you just might want to recruit in Salineville. I can tell you people understand loyalty, trust, good listening and genuine caring—foundations for a salesperson. Thanks Salineville.

From Marti and Rebecca...

To all of the amazing sales professionals in our lives—men and women, personal friends and clients—we offer a hearty "here's to you!" You've chosen a great profession. Thanks for generously sharing your stories so we could learn from and with you. We applaud your passion for selling, your tenacity to keep selling, and your willingness to try new approaches to make women your best, most loyal clients.

To our writer extraordinaire, Barry Schwenkmeyer, our heartfelt thanks for helping us find the right "voice". Your words, wisdom and wit are sure to inspire our readers.

To our extraordinary staff at Maddox Smye—you are simply the best. We couldn't have done it without your remarkable ability to support us and cheer us on at the same time.

To our loyal clients—who over the years have trusted us to teach and guide your sales people in new ways of relating and selling to their female clients. We celebrate your successes!

To our readers—writing this book has been a great adventure. The concepts and tools have been proven over and over in countless organizations across the United States and Canada. We only hope you will embrace the concepts and apply the tools. As always, we're solidly on your side! We promise you'll produce spectacular results.

INTRODUCTION

We're on YOUR Side

We need to say right up front that we are biased. We are unabashedly on your side—the side of the automotive sales professional. We know that for you to grow sales, you will have to win the hearts, minds, and pocket-books of women.

This is not another book on marketing to women or teaching women to become better-educated consumers. Unfortunately, in spite of all the snazzy ads, beautiful brochures, and slick media spots aimed at females, women are not always buying. They're shopping. And in many cases they're leaving the dealership and taking their money with them.

Sometimes they tell you why they're not buying, and sometimes they leave you guessing. Well, we believe you deserve better than that. You are part of an industry that in little more than a century has created millions of jobs and changed the face of a nation and the world.

Today's automotive manufacturers feed our desires for products that are fun, sexy, and status symbols, as well as utilitarian and durable. On the road and off, we're hooked. The economy may slow us down for a while, but nothing can stop our love affair with cars and trucks—not congested highways, not concerns about pollution, and not diminishing resources. There's nothing like an auto show on any continent to get consumers' adrenalin flowing and bring out the crowds.

As someone who sells or leases cars and trucks, you realize that you are selling more than a product. Whether your customer is male or female, when you hand over the keys to that vehicle, you are creating or reinforcing an identity. You are not only satisfying a family necessity, you are fulfilling a personal dream.

While you do it every day, the whole car-buying process is unsettling to the rest of us. Most of us only buy a vehicle every four years. So, we're inexperienced when it comes to negotiating the deal. And because the bad reputation of the few has rubbed off on the many, we find it hard to trust you. In short, you get a bum rap from the get-go.

Add to that mix the all-powerful Internet. You've heard the phrase "A little knowledge is a dangerous thing"? Well, that goes double for the Internet. How many of your customers come in with a fist-full of data on invoice prices, dealer holdbacks, and accessory costs? How many do you catch calculating how much they're going to demand off the price before you've even had a chance to introduce yourself?

Yes, the world of selling cars has changed. It's frightening and changing. It presents a huge opportunity. We believe that the savviest sales professionals and their dealer principals will recognize the changing needs of their customers and will be successful by becoming trusted advisors—forming strong and lasting relationships.

This book is about that kind of selling, the kind of selling that helps you close sales to women customers—effectively, time after time. Our research over the past 15 years proves that selling to women is a skill that can be learned. We encourage you to try it. Each chapter contains proven, practical methods and tools.

The Gender Issue

Don't think as you read this book that it was written for men only. Actually, it is written for sales professionals—both men and women. Both will benefit from it, but in slightly different ways.

Today's sales professionals, men and women, have been immersed in traditional male-oriented sales approaches. Female salespeople have been required to adopt traditional sales methods to *get with the program.* And though times are changing, business cultures around the world are still predominantly male.

If you are a man reading this book, you will undoubtedly recognize some typical male responses to a woman's behavioral style. You'll gain important insights into a woman's way of thinking, connecting, listening, decision-making, and timing. And by using these insights to shape your behavior, you'll see amazing results in your ability to sell effectively to women.

If you are a woman reading this book, you will probably recognize yourself when it comes to the buying process. And you may find that you've learned a sales approach that is sabotaging your own innate ability to relate effectively with your female customers. You may need to unlearn old approaches as well as learn new tools and techniques.

But whether you are a male or female sales professional, we know that by practicing our approach, you will become RICH selling to women.

For Men ONLY

Now that we've said that... we do have one chapter for men only. It's Chapter 13, and it's for all you men who want to take the learning to the next level—not only to increase your sales to women, but to build richer relationships with the wonderful women in your life.

In what we call "Lucky Chapter 13," we will challenge you to translate your knowledge, skills, and techniques into actions that will change your relationships for a lifetime. Enjoy the journey!

IT'S A WHOLE NEW BALL GAME

Do you want to make more money than you have ever made before? Do you want to do it in a way that will make you the most respected person in the dealership? In the next few chapters we're going to give you the inside story on how to sell cars and trucks to the fast-growing but poorly served women's market.

As one market expert put it, the women's market is low-hanging fruit, ripe for the picking by anyone with the smarts and the courage to try new ways of selling.

Today's women have the power, the money, and the confidence to insist on buying products and services in the ways that work best for them. If you can't do business the way they want, they'll find someone who can. It's that simple.

> *The way most organizations are accustomed to selling is not in sync with the way most women want to buy.*

Two converging trends have created this market.

Trend 1: Women are Making More Big-ticket Purchases of Traditionally Male Products

Women have moved beyond their traditional shopping venues. They have moved onto what was once considered male turf and now make big-ticket purchases of products and services in

INDUSTRIES WITH GROWING FEMALE CLIENT BASE

Financial Planning / Stocks and Bonds / Mortgages and Equity Loans / Banking Services / Cars / Boats / Motorcycles / New Houses / Building Supplies / Furniture / Computers / Broadband, Satellite, and Cable Systems / Security Systems / Heating and Cooling Systems / Insurance

everything from building supplies to cars to financial services to electronics to heating and cooling systems.

At some point in the last five years, women became the major purchasers and/or purchase influencers of traditionally male-oriented products. Why? Because women started earning more money. Today, 31% of married women who work outside the home earn more than their spouses.

You already know that women make or control over 80% of all consumer-buying decisions. You live it every day. How many times have you heard the man say, *"She wants the gray interior not the black?"* or *"I want a truck, but she thinks the kids will be safer in a minivan?"*

But here are some statistics that might surprise you:

> ➤ Women buy half of all sports equipment.[1]
> ➤ Women accounted for over half of the $96 billion spent on electronics in 2003.[2]
> ➤ A third of all women consider themselves early adopters of cutting-edge technology.[3]
> ➤ More single women than single men buy houses.
> ➤ Women make up 48% of all investors in the stock market.[4]

Women's earnings have been increasing for some time. What's different now is that women have assets. They own stocks and bonds, CDs, and rental property.

---

[1] According to the National Sporting Goods Association, in 2005 women purchased 51.1 percent of team sports equipment, fitness equipment, and camping equipment.

[2] Study by the Consumer Electronics Association quoted in "Consumer Electronics Companies Woo Women," AP January 15, May Wong.

[3] "Consumer Electronics Companies Woo Women"

[4] Chapter 13: Women and Finance, from WOW statistics, Diversity *Best Practices/ Business Women's Network*, Washington DC

Trend 2: Women are Embracing Their D-gene

Remember when it was politically incorrect to imply that women and men were different in any but the most obvious ways? Remember when a woman who sold cars and trucks had to be one of the guys? When a woman would never wear a dress or skirt to work for fear that people might think she was—well, female? She had to talk football, and fishing, and know who won last year's World Series. In those days, when different often was translated to mean inferior, there were perfectly good reasons for women to downplay their gender distinctions.

Today, women not only admit that they are different from men, they insist that society recognize their differences. And this new-found insistence makes them more responsive to products, services, and sales approaches that take these differences into account. Automotive manufactures have focus groups to address women's wants and needs in everything from door handles designed to keep women from breaking their fingernails to compartments in consoles for purses.

In fact, women have become so secure about their differences from men that they can now laugh about them. Did you, for example, see the story that was circulated on the Internet recently about a new drug called Buyagra? It's a stimulant taken prior to shopping that increases the duration and amount of spending. And who was forwarding that joke? Why women, of course!

We've dubbed the biological and cultural differences between men and women the D-gene. The D-gene refers to differences in how men and women communicate, how they relate to other people, how they make decisions, how they evaluate situations, and how they buy.

In Chapter 3, "Decoding the D-Gene," we'll take a look at these differences. Although some are the product of social conditioning, you may be surprised to learn that many are indeed genetic. Yes, it is true that men are hard-wired to be men, and women are hard-wired to be women.

The un-decoded D-gene is often the reason some of life's charming little moments turn into some of life's big ugly moments. Consider, for example:

> ➤ A woman's willingness to ask directions versus a man's insistence on finding his own way
> ➤ A woman's interest in watching one TV show at a time versus a man's need to channel-surf
> ➤ A woman's interest in going shopping versus a man's interest in making a purchase

We all recognize these potential flash points, although we don't all leverage them as creatively as the woman we heard of recently who was making a purchase in a department store. As she reached into her purse for her wallet, the salesperson noticed a remote control device.

"Do you always carry your TV remote with you?" the salesperson asked.

"No," she replied, "but my husband refused to come shopping with me, so I figured this was the worst thing I could to do him without getting arrested."

What gives this story the ring of truth that makes both men and women laugh? The D-gene.

Please understand we're not claiming that one gender is better than the other. It's the D for different gene, not the B for better gene. And we're certainly not saying that men don't try to bridge the gap. It's just that if they haven't decoded the D-gene, the gap is virtually unbridgeable.

Take the man who was attending a marriage seminar with his wife. At one point the leader said that a good husband always knows his wife's favorite flower. Hearing this, the husband smiled, leaned over to his wife, gently touched her arm, and whispered proudly, "It's Pillsbury, isn't it?"

This guy was obviously sincere. He thought he'd gotten it, so what's the problem? Why the disconnect?

Right. It's the darn D-gene.

These lighter moments illustrate at a domestic level the problem we find in sales organizations throughout North America. In the world of car sales, even if you get it, can you do it? Can the automotive industry do it?

By now, most organizations have made progress in reaching out to women—a little in some cases, a lot in others. Even organizations that sell traditionally male products have figured out how to make their marketing communications appeal to women. As you know, every major car manufacturer has set aside resources devoted to women's needs, although how much of this effort is real and how much is PR is somewhat unclear.

Still, one of the most exciting recent products designed with women in mind was Volvo's YCC (Your Concept Car) vehicle. It was designed by and for women. And here's what the women came up with:

> ➤ A system that communicates with the dealership to check systems and schedule maintenance, so women don't have to lift the hood or make a phone call.

> ➤ Rear seats that can be folded up like theatre seats, because women use the backseat for carrying packages more often than for passengers.

> ➤ Seat covers and interior carpets that can be changed whenever the owner want to redecorate the car with a new color scheme.

> ➤ Sensors to determine whether there is enough room in a parallel parking spot and to help steer the car into the spot.

It remains to be seen how many of these concept-car features will make their way into production. What seems clear, however, is that we have come a long way from that 1955 lavender-and-pink Dodge with rosebud upholstery.

Despite changes in the design process and marketing campaigns, it's remarkable that the way sales organizations sell to women has remained virtually unchanged. Whatever sensitivity about women's issues exists in the executive suite or the marketing department hasn't seemed to trickle down to the sales force. They still use pretty much the same spiel and the same techniques they did when most of their customers were men.

This is puzzling, because in terms of customer impact, selling is where the rubber hits the road. Nevertheless, few salespeople know the specifics of a woman's buying process. Of those who do, fewer still can translate their awareness into effective female-focused selling behaviors.

There is a huge gulf between what we know we *should* do and our ability to actually do it, especially when the stakes are high. It's one thing for a company to celebrate women and put out female-focused marketing materials. It's another thing for a sales force to learn female-friendly selling behaviors well enough to use them consistently and effectively with women.

> *Nowhere does an organization reveal its attitude towards women more vividly than in the behavior of its sales force.*

Behavioral change isn't easy, and it doesn't happen overnight. Take a look at any sport, and you'll see what we mean. Golfers know you're supposed to keep your head down when you make a shot, right? So why don't they always do it?

Well, for starters, it's because golf swings are like Archie Bunker's recliner and our favorite jeans. They are familiar and comfortable. It takes courage to set aside old ways or to try new approaches, especially when the old ways worked for us in the past. It also takes willingness to practice and a realization that to reach new levels of success you may have to go through a period of feeling a little awkward.

You know this. How many times have you heard someone say, "I paid $100 for that lesson with the pro, and it's really screwed up my swing!" And what does the golfer do? He goes back to his comfortable old swing and never improves.

We are here to tell you that your opportunities for success with this new market are more than worth the effort. We believe that the auto industry's traditional male-oriented selling practices are the major stumbling block in its attempt to engage successfully with women customers. If you update your selling practices, your sales numbers will increase. It's as simple as that.

WHAT THIS BOOK CAN DO FOR YOU

So here's the deal. The people who will get women's business will be those who take the trouble to decode the D-gene in the context of the cars and trucks they sell and adapt their behaviors accordingly. Using the concepts in this book, you will be able to create sales experiences for your women customers that are uniquely tailored to their needs and preferences.

MORE THAN / LESS THAN

When you sell to women, you do some things the same and some things differently. Mostly you do things more than or less than you would with your male customers.

We will tell you what most women won't— or can't:

> ➤ What women want at every point in a sales relationship
> ➤ What turns them off—immediately, and over time
> ➤ When to pursue, and when to back off
> ➤ How to encourage women to communicate their concerns directly to you, instead of broadcasting them to all their friends
> ➤ How to read the subtle cues that let you know how women are responding

Selling successfully to women does not require you to set aside everything you have ever learned about selling. You'll be able to stay within the guidelines of your existing selling process. As you become more effective, you may find yourself using these concepts with men as well as women customers.

Decoding the D-gene will pay off in several ways:

➤ Fewer women walking out the door
➤ Larger sales to women, including those big-ticket luxury and safety packages
➤ Repeat sales to your female customers
➤ Increased referrals from your women customers to their friends
➤ Higher scores on the customer satisfaction surveys
➤ More success with your male customers and prospects
➤ An improvement in your relationships with the women in your life

Ready for a sales-skills test drive to see if you need to learn new skills when it comes to selling more vehicles to women? Look at the following charts and see how you're doing?

Do you...	Then this book will...
1. Consider yourself already successfully selling to women?	Help you build on your success with some new tips and techniques.
2. Strive to treat male and female customers basically the same?	Increase your rate of success by showing you exactly how and under which circumstances women appreciate being treated differently.
3. Deal with your female customers by trying to be "softer" and avoiding performance data?	Demonstrate steps that create the difference between so-so results and get-rich success.

Do you...	Then this book will...
4. See women customers as mysteries; you never know where you stand with them, and are happy simply to avoid being offensive?	Give you the confidence to create successful sales strategies specifically designed with your women customers in mind.
5. Think most women suffer from male gender envy?	Challenge your thinking—enough, perhaps, to blast you out of your cave and into some successful sales to women.

And remember, if you're a female salesperson, we're giving you permission to tap into your D-gene and use it to make strong and profitable connections with your women customers.

A FINAL WORD

Throughout these pages you may take issue with some statements about the differences between men and women. "Wait a minute!" you might say. "I know plenty of women who don't behave—or think or feel—that way and plenty of men who do!"

We do too. We recognize that all of us live on a continuum of human behavior with many areas of overlap and very few hard-and-fast divisions. Not all women like to shop, for example, just as not all men refuse to ask for directions. However, as general statements these differences describe most men and women, and we stand by them.

In the final analysis, of course, an effective salesperson needs to go beyond generalities to respond to each customer as a unique individual with a unique set of needs.

We believe that the insights and advice we offer here will help you do just that—move beyond the barriers of gender differences to establish profitable, long-term relationships with your female customers.

2 THE WOMEN'S MARKET FOR CARS AND TRUCKS

ON THE ONE HAND, GOOD NEWS

As a sales professional in the auto industry, you already know that more and more women are buying cars. The percentage of car sales to women has exploded from 20 percent of all sales in 1984 to over 52 percent in 2004.[1] That 52 percent figure translates into $373 billion. To paraphrase former Senator Everett Dirksen, "A billion here. A billion there. Pretty soon we're talking real money!" The women's market for cars and trucks is huge.

And while we're talking numbers, let's look at a few more:

➤ Women account for 40 percent of the purchases of SUVs and light trucks. In fact, women today are buying every kind of car under the sun, and at every price point.[2]

➤ Women spend more than $300 billion annually on used car sales, maintenance, repairs, and service.[3] Over half of all used car sales are made to women

➤ In addition to direct purchases, women are estimated to influence the purchase of 95 percent of all vehicles sold in the U.S.[4]

[1] NADA DATA 2005, p. 41
[2] Rebecca Maddox, Presentation to Philadelphia Lincoln-Mercury dealers, 11/3/04.
[3] *Road & Travel Magazine* 2004.
[4] *Road & Travel Magazine*

There's no big secret to this surge; it's the same in many other traditionally male markets. Women today are living independently, supporting themselves and their families, moving into the world, and taking charge of their lives. Women's salaries may not yet have achieved parity with men's, but don't kid yourself, women today are making some serious money. They are building assets and are an economic force to be reckoned with. For example:

➤ Women own 40 percent of all U.S. businesses.
➤ 31 percent of all married working women earn more than their husbands.[5]
➤ Women head 40 percent of households with assets of over $600,000.

We could go on, but you get the picture.

There's also evidence that women car and truck buyers make better customers than men:

➤ Women customers will talk to their friends and family members more than men will about their experiences. A satisfied woman customer is a veritable referral machine.
➤ Women make up about 65 percent of an automotive service center's customer base.[6]
➤ Women typically are more loyal customers than men. Once you earn a woman's trust, she will tend to give you the benefit of the doubt more often than a man will. So if she's been treated well, she'll be less likely to defect to an outside repair shop once her vehicle's warranty expires.

Fueling this expansion of the market is the Internet, and the extensive product and pricing information available with just a

---

[5] Bureau of Labor Statistics.
[6] National Institute for Automotive Service Excellence

few clicks of the keyboard. Women, especially, appreciate the stronger buying position that Internet access has given them. Today, in fact, more than 5 percent of all new-vehicle sales are completed on the Internet, and 65 percent of all car buyers use one or more web sites to research and compare models, features, and costs.[7] As a result:

> Women arrive at a dealership much less susceptible to manipulation by salespeople who like to take advantage of a buyer's ignorance.

> Because she has done her homework, by the time a woman gets to the showroom she knows much more about what she wants, and is, therefore, closer to closing on a specific car at a specific price.

> When a woman can communicate with sellers via email, she knows she can avoid getting trapped by a high-pressure sales pitch.

> Having researched manufacturers' and dealers' costs, women are more knowledgeable about what constitutes a fair and realistic profit for a salesperson.

BUT ON THE OTHER HAND

The expansion of the women's market is indeed good news. Now, here's the not-so-good news, and something you may not know: According to a recent survey, *75 percent of all women say they will bring a man along for their next vehicle purchase just so they can get a fair deal.*[8]

PUT YOURSELF IN HER SHOES

Imagine you're trying to buy a carpet in a country where you don't speak the language. You don't know much about carpets, or local bargaining customs. Ask yourself how you would feel. Would you want to go back?

[7] John Gartner, "Car Dealers Feel Net Effect," *Wired News,* June 11, 2004
[8] Capital One Survey of Automotive Buying Habits, 2004

It doesn't take a genius to figure out what this says about a woman's typical car-buying experience. Is it accurate? Who cares? Three-quarters of today's women *think* it's accurate, and that's what's important.

Although most people enter a dealership with some excitement, they often end up in an adversarial relationship. Three out of four women walk out saying, "Never again."

WHAT YOUR WOMEN CUSTOMERS AREN'T TELLING YOU

If a woman customer feels she is being treated badly and tells you about it, consider yourself lucky. At least you know what the problem is, and stand a fighting chance of fixing it. More often, women will say nothing, find a graceful way to leave, and never come back. They don't have the time to get into it, they don't like to be confrontational, and they figure that no matter what they say, you're a lost cause. But guess what? Even if they don't tell you, they'll tell 20 of their friends. That's the power of female networking, and we'll show you how you can put it to positive use later in the book.

So, just so you'll know, here are the common complaints women make about the people who try to sell them cars, starting the moment they drive onto the lot.

> ➤ *"Before you're even out of your car, they're right there looming over you. It's intimidating and most women resent it."*

> ➤ *"A salesman will ask a woman if he can help her. If she says no, he doesn't know what to do, so he just hovers behind her as she walks around the showroom. It's quite a sight: she's trying to ignore him and he is trying to figure out what to say."*

➤ *"I told him I'm a biker and the most important thing for me was how a bike rack would fit on the car. He says, 'Maybe I can look into that,' and goes right on with his standard pitch."*

➤ *"I hate it when they get cute with the price. They say that's their best price, but then they call back later and say if you find a better price somewhere else maybe they can come down. That's when I stop trusting them."*

"Before I go car-shopping," said one experienced woman, "I try to work up some 'attitude.' You've got to fight fire with fire."

➤ *"One salesman really pressured me to close on my first visit. He did everything but tie me to the chair and make me sign."*

➤ *"I'm asking the questions, but he's directing the answers to my husband, even though my husband keeps telling him I'm the buyer."*

➤ *"He actually forgets my name, or calls me by the wrong name."*

➤ *"If I'm going to buy a $40,000 product," said one woman who had been in a dealership where the salesmen dressed sloppily and wore baseball hats, "I expect the salesperson to be dressed for the occasion."*

➤ *"He gave me a sob story about how I had to give him perfect customer service ratings so he could get his full commission."*

➤ *"He kept trying to uncover the 'real' decision-maker, meaning my husband."*

➤ *"When my husband brought my car in for service, they gave him a loaner. They had never given me a loaner."*

➤ *"He told me my car would be ready at a certain time, and didn't seem all that bothered when it wasn't. I guess he assumed I didn't have anything else to do."*

➤ *"As soon as he made the sale, he never heard of me."*

Some salespeople assume that these are complaints made by other people's customers. They know that *their* female customers are perfectly satisfied. What they don't realize is that women, especially older women, are so accustomed to adapting themselves to men that it would never occur to them to complain—even in buying situations where they hold the power of the purse.

But although they haven't told you, they've told 20 of their friends and any number of women in the supermarket checkout line. Their experiences have been so unpleasant that 75 percent of women say they're going to even up the odds next time they buy a vehicle by taking a man along with them to run interference.

THE FIELD IS WIDE OPEN

What we're saying is that the women's market for cars and trucks is yours for the taking—if you can become the kind of sales professional who always gives women customers a fair deal even if they don't bring a man along. If you become known as a salesperson who deals with women on their own terms— who really takes in what they tell you, gets them what they are looking for, and provides all the support and information they want both during and after the sale—you will CLEAN UP.

In this book we're going to tell you how.

It doesn't take a Ph.D. in psychology to understand this. Think about your own reactions. If you had the choice, would you buy from a salesperson who ignored, patronized, and intimidated you? Someone who you believe would talk you into a deal you suspect is a rip-off? Or would you prefer to work with a salesperson who takes the time to understand you and what you want, and does everything possible to make sure you're satisfied? Need we say more?

And the good news is, at least at this point in time, that by treating women the way they want to be treated, you will have an advantage over all the other guys who are still using the same old techniques.

Wait a minute, we can hear you thinking, "Hasn't the automotive world become more aware of women?" Well, yes and no. Yes, there are more female automotive executives. There are more marketing programs aimed at a woman. There are more female-friendly car features.

Unfortunately, these corporate efforts seldom affect the selling behaviors of the salespeople in the showroom—which is precisely where women confront the company and experience the greatest difficulties. That's where this book comes in. We will show you how to adapt the way you sell to the way women want to buy.

AND SMART SALESPEOPLE ALSO MAKE THE INTERNET WORK FOR THEM

What salespeople don't always realize is that the Internet is a big boon for people who know how to use it.

➤ The more customers get information about a vehicle from the Internet, the more time the salesperson can devote to developing good customer relationships. As you'll see in this book, this approach is especially successful with women customers.

➤ When customers can make initial queries via email, salespeople are more likely to get customers in the showroom who are interested in buying, not just kicking tires. "We close on 40 percent of customers who come in via the Internet," said the manager of a Midwestern dealer, "versus 22 percent of walk-ins."

➤ When customers come in knowing what they want to buy and how much they want to spend, salespeople on the showroom floor can close faster. Faster closes can translate into more sales.

What prevents salespeople from seizing the benefits of the Internet is out-dated selling behavior, and the all-too-human reluctance to adapt to change. A woman customer told us about coming into a showroom after shopping the dealership on the Internet. She was directed to a salesman. His first words to her were an impatient: "So, how many other dealers did you contact, and what price do I have to beat?" Suffice it to say, she didn't give him the opportunity to beat anyone's price!

When push comes to shove, even those salespeople who recognize the need will often resist trying new approaches. They talk about it, and they know they should do something different, but they don't know what. As one seasoned salesperson put it, "It's all upside down now. All our cost information is right out there for anyone who wants it. What other business is that true for?"

Today the best dealers and the best salespeople realize that developments like the Internet and the growth of the women's market call for new ways of selling. Some use specially trained people to answer customer e-mail queries and make sales appointments. Others have actual Internet sales departments. It requires change—new ways of thinking and new ways of relating to the customer. And the women's market is well worth the effort required to make those changes.

IT'S THE RELATIONSHIP

In this book we will tell you what to do every step of the way to successfully sell cars and trucks to women, but here's a headline: It all boils down to relationships. If you want to sell successfully to women, you need to know how to develop and maintain thoughtful, creative, honest, and proactive long-term relationships with women.

Yes, we know, everyone tries to develop relationships with his or her customers. The relationships we're talking about, however, are different from the kinds of relationships you may have with male customers. These are a little deeper, a little more "human," and a lot less cut-and-dried. They call for a new understanding and new behaviors. You'll probably need to pay a little more attention, be a little more creative, and share a lot more of yourself

Having a trusting relationship with you is more important to a female than to a male customer.

than you are used to. And we don't mean in a canned speech about the facts of your life ("Well, I'm married with two children, and I've been here 14 years, and…"), but in smaller moments that enable you to establish common ground and let her know the kind of a person you are ("I know what you mean. If a restaurant is too noisy, I don't care how good the food it.")

THE POWER OF THE PAST

Before we go any further, a few things need to be said about the history that most women bring to the dealer showroom—and indeed to any big-ticket purchase in a male-oriented business or industry. You probably won't hear these from your women customers, but if you want to be successful selling to them, you need to know about them.

As we said, women see the auto business as male-oriented. For whatever reasons, they have always associated everything about cars—building them, driving them, repairing them, racing them, buying them—with boys and men. Small wonder that a dealership's selling practices are also male-oriented. Therefore, before we tell you how you can adapt these selling practices to the way women like to buy, we need to talk about the power of this perceived male orientation, because it exerts a strong influence on a woman's expectations and concerns when she thinks about doing business with you—way before she walks in the door.

When a woman goes to buy a car, she feels on a conscious or unconscious level that she's going to be playing a man's game and will, therefore, be at a disadvantage. This is true even though:

➤ She may feel confident and assertive in other areas.

➤ She may be wealthy and financially sophisticated, as more and more women are today.

➤ She may have a high-powered job.

➤ She may manage her own business and/or family finances.

➤ She may be working with a woman salesperson.

In the back of her mind, there still lurks the feeling that she's operating in foreign territory, even though she may not be aware of this feeling until something happens to trigger it.

Ironically, a wife may experience this most keenly when she's in the dealer's showroom with her husband—whom she probably brought along to get a fair deal—and the three of them are talking about a car.

> *To be successful with women, it's not enough to be good at your job. You also have to be good as a person. This means being honest, having integrity, and consistently doing the right thing.*

Perhaps the conversation began as a three-way interaction, but soon the salesman is trading sports statistics with the husband, and briefing him on various performance issues he assumes the wife either can't understand or won't be interested in. (How much the husband actually understands is another story.) Later on, when the couple doesn't return his calls, he wonders why he didn't get their business.

If you're a man, you may have a hard time imagining how alienated and powerless this treatment can make a woman feel. If you've ever made a purchase in a lingerie shop, you may have felt awkward and a little silly—but that's different from feeling patronized and excluded.

Women have antennae that unfailingly pick up all kinds of details, and will spot the slightest indication of condescension or patronizing behavior a mile away—even if you didn't intend it. They can tell when the details don't add up. There may be brochures and posters on every wall trumpeting the dealership's commitment to women, but for the woman its true degree of commitment emerges in how she is treated in face-to-face interactions.

Because a man might not take such treatment personally, you may find a woman's reaction hard to understand. Perhaps you think she is being overly sensitive; but if you want to succeed as a sales professional, you need to do everything in your power to avoid sending signals indicating you're giving her anything less than your total respect and attention.

THE OTHER SIDE OF THE COIN

What complaints do salespeople have about their female customers? Here are some typical comments:

> *I never know where I stand with them.* "If I make a presentation to a guy, and he doesn't buy, I figure, 'Oh well, win some, lose some.' With a woman, I always wonder, 'Did I do something wrong? Did I offend her in some way?'"

> *They pay more attention to their friends than they do to me.* "They've got this whole network of relatives and friends giving advice. And of course they assume I'm lying to them."

> *They tell me their life stories.* "I mean, OK, she's got a teenager and a granddaughter living at home, and her husband is out of work, and on and on. Meanwhile the clock is ticking and the sale is going nowhere."

> ➤ *They ask too many questions.* "Women can get so intense. The more I tell them, the more they ask me. It's like they're trying to cover any possible eventuality. Some of that's a good thing, but lighten up, is what I say."

> ➤ *They take too long to make decisions.* "I'll call her—you know, check in to see where she is. But I get the feeling she doesn't want to be pressured, so now I don't know how to move things along. We could both be dead before she decides."

THE IRONY OF THE SITUATION

If you look at what the salespeople say, it's all about women not fitting into the traditional way the salespeople are used to doing business. Women take too long, talk too much, and ask too many questions.

Women's complaints, on the other hand, center on the lack of a personal relationship. Agents don't listen. They're not friendly. They treat customers impersonally. They don't return calls.

The irony is that, despite all the salespeople's complaints, the research demonstrates that women are more disposed than men to listen to people they perceive as trustworthy experts. Also, women are more loyal than men. Once a woman feels she can trust you, she'll stay with you. A man, on the other hand, is more focused on the deal. If he can get a better deal elsewhere, he's likely to move on.

Products and services eventually become commodities. The only lasting competitive advantage lies in human interaction.

If, as a car or truck sales professional, you want to tap into the enormous women's market, the message is clear: you need to spend at least as much time establishing trusting relationships with your women customers as you do developing your product savvy and technical expertise. The secret lies in your ability to adapt what you do to the needs and preferences of your women customers throughout a sale—from the critical initial minutes of a first meeting to the sale's close; from service and support after the sale to maintaining an ongoing relationship that will produce additional leads and sales in the future.

And how do you do this? The first step is learning how to decode the D-gene. That's the topic of the next chapter.

DECODING THE D-GENE

What are the differences between men and women, and why should you care about them? So far we've been talking about the D-gene in general terms. Now it's time to get specific.

In this chapter we will concentrate on the four areas of male-female differences that have the greatest impact on the buying and selling process:

➤ How men and women relate to other people
➤ How they express themselves
➤ How they take in and process information
➤ How they make decisions

This is the information you need to maximize your sales to women. It can mean the difference between striking out (or making a one-time sale) and creating loyal customers who trust you to do what's best for them over the long haul.

WHERE DO THE DIFFERENCES COME FROM?

Are women different than men because of their genetic make-up or because of how they were raised? There's no simple answer to this nature-nurture debate, although recent research seems to be swinging the pendulum towards nature. In other words, when you forbid your young son to play with toy guns, and you find he's chewed a piece of toast into the shape of a pistol and is systematically taking out imaginary intruders, it just may be because he's male.

Men and women are biologically different. The male-female differences that developed many thousands of years ago to ensure the survival of our species are still imprinted on our genes. Men are still wired to be hunters and women are still wired to be nurturers. Now, does that mean that women stay home and bake cookies while men go out and design, engineer, manufacture and sell cars? Of course not. Today everyone knows that women can be successful breadwinners, and men can stay home and raise healthy, happy children.

> **BLAME IT ON THE D-GENE #2**
>
> *Why do women always have the last word?*
>
> *Because anything a man says after that becomes the beginning of the next argument.*

Nevertheless, some significant male-female differences remain, stronger in some individuals than in others. They are at the root of the tension between the sexes that people often defuse through humor: he won't ask for directions and she won't keep quiet during the football game. When it comes to selling successfully to women, however, these differences deliver more than just a few laughs. Once you understand them, you have the keys to the sales kingdom.

Our purpose here is to help you increase your sales. It would be a mistake at this point to veer off into an argument over which differences are better. There is no better or worse, there is only different. The only point we want to make is that a sales professional can use this understanding to address the preferences of women customers—and as a result to achieve greater success in terms of initial sales, loyal customers, repeat business, and referrals.

LET'S TALK ABOUT HORMONES

Don't worry. This is not a biology lecture, but any discussion of the D-gene has got to start with *hormones.* Most people know that testosterone is the male hormone, and estrogen the primary female hormone, although women have some testosterone, and men have some estrogen.

> **RELATIONSHIP-ORIENTED FROM THE GET-GO**
>
> *Female infants sustain eye contact twice as long as boys. They're also better at distinguishing between photos of people they know and people they don't.*

> ➤ *Testosterone* is what makes men strong, competitive, aggressive, and inclined to take risks. Research tells us that testosterone also contributes to such other traits as math and analytical ability, mechanical skills, and a talent for navigating and reading maps. (There is no indication that it facilitates operation of a television remote control.) These qualities were vital in the days when men had to compete for and keep mates, hunt for food, and protect their families against danger.

> ➤ *Estrogen* is the female equivalent of testosterone. It increases a woman's interest in nest-building and nurturing. Another hormone, progesterone, triggers the maternal feelings she needs to bond with her infant. Oxytocin, which helps induce labor, also facilitates mother-and-child bonding. In fact, during some moments of stress, when men release the adrenaline that produces the "fight or flight" syndrome, women release oxytocin, which drives them to seek safety and solace with others, a response that is sometimes referred to as the tend and befriend response. In fact, researchers now believe that oxytocin helps women form healthy interpersonal relationships of all kinds.

> ➤ Researchers also believe that women's higher levels of the hormone *serotonin* reduce their aggression and interest in risk-taking activities.

A woman's interest in forming emotional connections with other people is permanent and deep-seated. This is why it's so important to establish a trustworthy relationship with your woman customers. It is also why they are turned off by hardball competition and negotiations that underlie many sales to men.

AND THEN THERE'S THE BRAIN

A woman's brain is indeed wired differently than a man's. Men's brains tend to have clearly separated functions. Women's brains, by and large, tend to have more internal connections, within and across hemispheres. Women's emotional centers, for example, are found in many parts of the brain, while men's are concentrated in the right side. This interconnected distribution may support a broader, more nonlinear thinking style in a woman, in contrast to a man's more focused approach.

Remember this difference while you listen to a woman tell you what she's looking for in a car or truck. Know that she's going to jump from her need for four-wheel drive, to driving five kids to soccer, to airbags, to having a place for her purse, to getting her aged parents in and out of the back seat—all in the same breath! It's simply her way of processing information—one thought leads to another.

This drives men nuts. They want to approach each subject, from transverse engine mounts, to front-wheel versus all-wheel drive, to the whistles and bells, one at a time. As a male salesperson, you can use this understanding to relate to your women customers. Rather than showing your impatience with her rambling, tune into her different thinking style. Pay attention and you'll find you can listen attentively and with respect. The payoff for you is that you'll gain valuable information—and you'll earn her trust and loyalty.

EXPECTATIONS OF SOCIETY

Society is part of the *nurture* component that increases differences between men and women. Although the gap between the *rules* for males and females has certainly narrowed in the last 40 years, there is still plenty of social pressure on women and girls to act in traditionally female ways. They are still expected to be relatively quiet, compliant, polite, and controlled. Consider the common reaction to a woman who loses her temper, speaks up strongly in public, or interrupts when someone else is speaking.

As a sales professional, make sure not to unwittingly play into these pressures by making your customer fight to get her point across. Avoid assuming that her silence means agreement, and encourage her, without harassing her, to speak up.

THE D-GENE AND SELLING TO WOMEN

Armed with this quick background, let's return to the four sales-related areas where the D-gene has the biggest impact, and take a look at what you can do to accommodate your sales approach to women's preferred buying process.

As you read, think about your current sales habits. Is the way you sell tailored primarily to men? Do you see places where you might modify it to make your women customers more comfortable?

Again, keep in mind that we are talking about most men and most women. Don't get hung up on the people you may know who behave differently. Once you get the overall model, you can tweak your approach to fit people who exhibit a combination of male and female characteristics.

How Men and Women Relate to Other People

Men typically see themselves as independent operators who relate to others by achieving goals and solving problems. A strong element of competition is often involved. Women tend to see themselves in the context of their relationships, based on establishing and sharing emotional connections.

For example:

Women	Men
Woman are relationship-oriented. They derive identity from their place in relationships.	Men are transaction-oriented. They derive identity from what they do and achieve.
Women are conditioned to get along, be nice. They work to ensure win/win outcomes. They like to share, equalize, work together. They see themselves as part of a culture of equals.	Men are raised on and comfortable with competition and win/lose outcomes. A man sees himself as part of a hierarchy, with some people above and some below him. Men are more comfortable in a command-and-control environment.
Women thrive on courtesy and respect. Politeness and manners, insofar as they build bridges and avoid conflict, mean a lot to them. The closer competition gets to overt conflict, the more uncomfortable women become with it.	Men thrive on competition. They see negotiation as a challenging game in which they can test their skills and perhaps dominate the other person. Their physical contact with other men is often rough and jostling.
A woman's style is to create community, brainstorm with others, build consensus.	A man's style is to dominate, interrupt, give advice, and do more telling than asking.
Women tend to be open to the input and influence of others.	Men resist being influenced by others. They prefer to be seen as making up their own minds.

SELLING TIPS

Whatever you can do to establish and maintain a relationship with a woman customer will make her feel more comfortable, and therefore more likely to buy from you. Establishing a connection should be your primary goal. If you do that, the sale will almost take care of itself. To build a relationship:

> **BLAME IT ON THE D-GENE #3**
>
> **Men at lunch:** *When a bill for $52.50 arrives, each of the four guys will throw in a twenty. None will have anything smaller—and no one will admit to wanting any change back.*
>
> **Women at lunch:** *When the bill arrives, out come the pocket calculators.*

➤ Find commonalities in your lives—children, hobbies, favorite authors, travel —and share them. Remember to bring them up whenever you talk.

➤ Look for opportunities to share your feelings. That's right, feelings. Let's face it, you'll never create a strong personal bond by discussing engine torque. The more you open up, the more she'll trust you. Don't be afraid to ask about her thoughts and feelings, either.

➤ Introduce her to the people at the dealership whom she may work with at some point. Let her know that these people are important to you and to her. They are part of your team, and therefore also part of her team.

➤ Host gatherings that bring together your women customers and/or prospects. Make sure that these events are small enough for people to get to know one another.

How Men and Women Express Themselves

Did you know that women talk more than men? In one study women clocked in at 25,000 words a day while men uttered a mere 12,000. Men think women talk primarily to transmit information. Wrong. That's what men do. Women talk to gather information, connect, check on and maintain relationships, find their place in a group, and feel safe.

For example:

Women	Men
Women like communication with more context, emotional content, and detail. They tend to tell the whole story, starting at the beginning.	Men like communication that is concise, streamlined, and often focused on specific actions or results.
Women value communication as a way to interact, express emotions and offer intuitions.	Men value communication as a way to give and receive information, discover and express facts.
Women talk more often in terms of preferences and suggestions. They ask more question than men.	Men talk more often in terms of information and advice. They ask fewer questions.
Women's language is characterized by disclaimers ("I'm no expert, but...") and qualifiers ("Don't you think we should..."). They make fewer direct statements than men.	Men's language is more direct, with fewer qualifiers than women. It's also characterized by teasing, joking, and verbal bantering.
Women tend to disclose personal information about themselves as part of establishing connections with others.	Men tend not to disclose personal information. It's their way of protecting their independence, and keeping their options open.
Women make eye contact while talking with another person.	Men make less eye contact while talking with others.
Women interrupt less. They also allow more interruptions, although they don't *like* being interrupted.	Men interrupt more, and allow fewer interruptions.

SELLING TIPS

➤ Don't waste your time trying to cut a woman off, or hurry her story along. She won't like it, and besides, it won't work. The fact is, if you know how to listen, everything a woman says is golden. If you pay attention to what she says, you'll eventually be able to offer products and services that fit perfectly into her life, including some she may not even know she needs.

> **BLAME IT ON THE D-GENE #4**
>
> *"Of course we talk more than men," one woman said. "We have to say everything twice because men don't listen."*

➤ Don't assume that just because she doesn't always cut to the chase, she doesn't know what she wants. Women soften assertions with various qualifiers. They pepper their conversations with words like *mostly, maybe, possibly,* and *sometimes.* It's a mistake to assume that because she uses these phrases she's not serious or well-informed.

➤ Maintain eye contact. If you're a man, this might feel awkward at first; when men talk, they tend not to look at each other as much as women do. To a woman, not looking her in the eye makes you seem shifty and untrustworthy.

➤ Don't interrupt. Or, to put it another way: DON'T INTERRUPT! For men, interrupting and being interrupted are part of the normal give-and-take of a conversation. The better the conversation, the more interruptions. Not so for a woman. Women wait their turn. Nothing makes a woman feel more irritated or discounted than being interrupted. You may know where her conversation is heading. You may know exactly what she needs. You may have an exciting idea you just can't wait to present. Forget about it. Bite your tongue until it's bloody, if you need to, but... don't interrupt.

How Men and Women Take In and Process Information

Think of a funnel with information going in the top and coming out the bottom. With a woman, the funnel stays wider longer and takes in a greater variety of information. With a man, it narrows sooner, discarding extraneous data earlier along the way.

For example:

Women	Men
Women see themselves as students. They're comfortable asking for help and admitting what they don't know.	Men see themselves as masters of a situation. They're less comfortable asking for help and admitting what they don't know.
Women think more concretely, often organizing information into stories.	Men think more abstractly. They look for principles, rules, patterns.
When applying the rules, women are often more interested in the person's circumstances than in an abstract notion of good and bad. They use their own experiences and examples to make decisions.	Men often see situations in abstract terms of right and wrong, good and bad. They are more likely than women to think that the rules should be applied equally to everyone.
Women listen actively and physically—nodding, smiling, gesturing.	Men listen passively. Often they show little or no response at all.
Women nod to indicate they are listening.	Men nod to indicate agreement.
Women are more sensitive than men to body language, emotional states, and nonverbal cues.	Men tend to focus on the objective facts.
Women seek to *expand* their perspective and search out options.	Men tend to analyze, sifting through facts to *eliminate* those that don't apply so they can zero in on the key points.

SELLING TIPS

➤ Do less lecturing. With women disposed to listen and ask questions, and men disposed to see themselves as experts, the temptation to pontificate can be powerful, if you are a man. Resist it at all costs.

➤ Tell more stories when you talk about your products. Make sure your stories apply to her goals, her needs, her family, her future. It's all about her.

➤ LISTEN. This, of course, is the flip side of DON'T INTERRUPT!

➤ *Show* that you're listening. Nod, say "mm-hmm." Inject a response from time to time to let her know you're tracking. Remember, a woman can usually spot someone who is only pretending to listen.

How Men and Women Make Buying Decisions

For a woman, purchasing something that is a traditionally male item will almost always be a high-stakes decision, regardless of the cost of the product. Along with her lack of experience in the area, and a concern that she may be taken advantage of, she does not want to get home and have her husband or boyfriend say, "They really sold you a bill of goods! How much did you pay⸮!"

Women shop. Men buy.

For example:

Women	Men
Women feel a need to make the "perfect" or "right" decision.	Men are generally satisfied with a "good" decision.
Women tend to buy a relationship. They are influenced by how they're treated.	Men tend to buy a product. They are influenced by the deal they got.

Women	Men
A woman often begins the buying process by talking with others she knows who are knowledgeable. (However, when it comes to researching vehicles, women are enthusiastic Internet users.)	Men tend to begin the process with independent research.
A woman's buying process encompasses a circular search pattern, involving thinking, discussing, comparing, and collaborating. For her, a purchase is about the process.	A man's buying process is more linear—from research to the purchase. For him, it's about solving a problem.
Women express interest in what a product or service does for them and for those who matter to them.	Men express interest in a product's or service's efficiencies, and how it works.
Women take longer to decide, but in the end are more loyal clients.	Men make quicker decisions, but are fickle and less loyal.

SELLING TIPS

➤ Be patient. Don't indicate in any way that she's taking too long to make up her mind. (And don't forget that women are experts at reading body language.)

➤ Prepare yourself for second, third, and fourth opinions. A woman who wants to buy a car will seek advice from everyone she knows. And each person will have his two cents to add. You may be irritated at having so many opinions to respond to, but there isn't much you can do about it.

➤ Keep the relationship uppermost in your mind, because she certainly will. You may have shown her every car on the lot, but if you don't return her calls promptly, she may not return yours—ever.

BLAME IT ON THE D-GENE #5

A woman asks her husband to help her shop for a dress for an upcoming cocktail party. "I was thinking of something red," she says.

As soon as they get to the store, he spots a red dress on the rack and says, "This looks nice. Why don't you try it on?"

When she comes out of the dressing room, she looks really great and he tells her so.

She agrees—which is why he's surprised when she insists they check out what other stores have to offer.

And at the end of the day, which dress does she buy? Right, the one they saw first.

What the husband thinks they did: waste their time.

What the wife thinks they did: research.

➤ Help her connect emotionally with the product by showing how it will make her life better. And make sure she knows how it will benefit the lives of those she cares about.

Now that you know about the D-gene and what it can tell you, you're ready to apply this new knowledge to fine-tuning your overall selling approach.

NOT UNTIL SHE TRUSTS YOU

What Women Want Most in a Buying Experience

Research tells us that when it comes to making large purchases, men look first for value—the deal they're able to get. Next they decide whether they like the salesperson; finally, they look at whether this is someone they can trust.

> *"I felt manipulated towards a choice which had nothing to do with what I needed. I couldn't see how it would benefit me in any way."*

With women, it's exactly the opposite. Before anything else, a woman needs to trust the sales professional she's working with, especially in traditionally male industries. After trust comes likeability, and last comes the deal or value. In fact, women tend to see value emerging from the relationship. Research shows that a woman will pay up to 28 percent more for a product in order to buy it from someone she trusts and likes.

A woman is looking for clues that she can trust you the minute she walks in the door. (See Chapter 5, "The Two-Minute Takeoff.") If she picks up the slightest indication that she can't trust you, the game is over before it begins as far as the she is concerned.

What a woman seeks in a relationship with someone who's about to sell her a car or truck is different from what a man looks for. Both, obviously, want to know that you will live up to your word, and that you have their best interests at heart. A woman, however, has some additional requirements:

➤ Can she rely on the strength of a personal relationship with you?

➤ Can she trust you, as an ally, to understand the pressures in her life and to help her ease them?

➤ Can she expect special treatment from you, if she needs it—not because she is a special person (or not *only* because she is a special person), but because she may be short on both experience and time?

TRUST IS A FUNNY THING

Trust is a much-valued but often misunderstood quality. Ultimately, it's up to other people to decide whether you're trustworthy or not.

Here are a few things you need to know about trust:

➤ People make their decisions by carefully evaluating your behavior over time. Grand gestures may impress for the moment but are quickly forgotten if your behavior in the smaller moments is inconsistent. Again, trust takes time to grow.

WHAT ABOUT MEN?

Don't men like special treatment, too? Sure they do. But for women it plays a bigger part in a satisfying buying experience.

➤ Once people do trust you, they no longer need further proof of your trustworthiness. They will then take your word, follow your advice, and accept your recommendations.

➤ However—and this is a BIG however—it takes only a moment to break this trust, and a long, long time to earn it back.

THE 5 PRINCIPLES OF TRUST-BASED SELLING

We've organized everything you need to do to build trust with your women customers into five principles:

Think relationship before product.

Respect her, her time, and her timing.

Understand her on her own terms.

Surpass her every expectation.

Telegraph confidence.

If you can internalize these principles and use them to shape your behavior, you'll have women customers who will be open to your advice, stay with you through good times and bad, and tell so many of their friends how wonderful you are that you'll never run short of enthusiastic referrals.

1. Think relationship before product.

Because a woman relates more to people than to things, she finds it easier to connect with you than with the car or truck you're selling. To her, the sales relationship comes before the sale. Whereas a man is looking for the best deal, a woman is looking for a total buying experience. You'll earn her trust (and her business) if you take the time to invest in getting to know her and letting her get to know you. There will be plenty of time to share your extensive product knowledge once you've established a connection. So, slow down. Don't try to close the sale in the same time frame that might work with a man.

WHAT THIS MEANS FOR YOU

If you can pace yourself to accommodate her process, you'll avoid frustration, and she'll relax and begin to feel more comfortable doing business with you. If you look at the clock while working with her, she'll look for the door.

HOW TO BRIDGE THE D-GENE

The challenge for most salespeople—men and women alike—is to shift their initial focus away from what they're selling to building relationships with prospective customers. Although they may understand the importance of establishing a relationship, most salespeople do not realize just how human women customers need this relationship to be. Easy to say, but how do you do it? Here's how:

> ➤ *Allow time for her to get to know you—and you to get to know her.* When you're selling to a woman, be prepared for a process rather than an event. If you were taking a trip from Point A to Point B, the difference might be something like this: a man would get on an eight-lane interstate and be there in three hours. A woman would take the back roads and not arrive for two days. That's because she wants to experience the trip itself so she can get comfortable with the new territory.
>
> Much as you might like, you can't speed up her journey, so put it out of your mind. In the first place, if you spend all your time wishing she'd get on the interstate, a woman is going to pick up the vibe that you're rushing her, even if you don't say anything. Second, you're going to lose out on the chance not only to build a strong relationship, but to learn things about her that will help you tailor your selling process.

One car salesperson tells of the women who came in to buy a minivan. She said she needed it to carpool her daughter's swim team. As he listened and let her talk, he discovered that what she really wanted was a convertible. The dealership had just taken in a nice one on a trade. He showed her the minivan and the convertible. She bought both.

➤ *Establish common ground.* This is different from the male practice of checking each other out to see who went to the better college, earns the higher salary, or lives in the nicer neighborhood. With women, the point is to find commonalities that will help bring you together as equals.

Check to see what pastimes you share. Bring up community events she may have attended. See what she thinks of the new restaurant in town.

Don't be afraid to ask questions, but be careful not to sound like a prosecutor interrogating a hostile witness. Lead with personal information of your own, and see if she responds. Pets, children, and grandchildren resonate with almost everyone.

➤ *Notice what she may be carrying with her.* It could be a picture on a key chain, a travel brochure, or a book. Use it to create a connection. Say something like: "I couldn't help noticing the picture you have on your keychain. You must be a cat lover, too."

The key here is to be observant. With the exception of Sherlock Holmes and Lieutenant Columbo, men aren't known for having an abundance of this trait. But with practice, you'll be surprised how much you can pick up.

THIS OLD THING?

With greater powers of observation, you may even wise up to your spouse's habit of slipping new clothes past you. You know the one: "New? Oh no, Honey, I've had this dress for ages."

➤ *Remember her name and the names of the significant people in her life.* This may sound obvious, but it's especially important to women. If Julie calls you for some information, and you call her Jenny, she probably won't hang up on you, but you will definitely have lost some ground in earning her trust. On the other hand, if you can refer to her son or grandson by name, she will certainly think, and may even say, "Oh, you remembered!"

➤ *Act as her ally in the sales process.* Think of your dealership's sales process. Where are the potential bottlenecks? Where's the red tape? Where are problems likely to arise? Remember, she's a busy person, and will appreciate anything you can do to help expedite the process for her. So don't forget about her once you've made the sale. Help her understand what will happen next, and what additional paperwork she may need to deal with. Intercede on her behalf if a problem crops up. If she's looking for some kind of special arrangement, or an exception to one of your rules, see what you can do to accommodate her. Your efforts will pay off in her trust—and in future sales from her and her friends.

2. **Respect her, her time, and her timing.**

First, you can respect a woman customer by treating her with courtesy—not only the pull-her-chair-out-from-the-table kind but also the respectful deference that tells her she's the focus of your efforts. Second, you will never go wrong if you can always remember how short of time she is. By and large, women are a lot busier than men, especially working women. With their ability to multi-task, they are often given multiple responsibilities to juggle at work. And at home? Well, married working women still shoulder the bulk of family responsibilities. And being a single mom is not exactly a walk in the park.

WHAT THIS MEANS FOR YOU

Because it's so important for women to feel that they are being taken seriously, you can set yourself apart by going out of your way to extend respect. Quiet, focused forms of attention register big with women.

If you can support whatever decision-making approach your woman customer wants to use, whether it's asking lots of questions, conferring with friends and family members, or just taking her time, you'll earn her respect, gratitude and future business.

DEMON MULTI-TASKERS

*In the same time it takes the **husband** to make the morning coffee, the **wife** will fix breakfast, pack the kids' lunches, write a shopping list, iron a shirt, call the office, find missing homework, and de-flea the cat.*

HOW TO BRIDGE THE D-GENE

By now you may suspect that your biggest challenge as a sales professional might be dealing with a woman's busy schedule, on the one hand, and giving her the time she needs to make a decision, on the other. You might think that the solution would be to help her decide faster. Wrong. Here's a more effective approach:

➤ *Learn about her schedule and time frame for making decisions.* Be on time. When you're five or ten minutes late for a meeting with a male customer, it's not good, but it's not the end of the world. A woman, on the other hand, may have planned her day so closely that she can't afford to lose ten minutes. She may be paying a dollar for every minute she's late picking up her kid at child care. More important for your relationship with her, a woman is much more likely than a man to take your lateness personally. She may think you don't respect her enough to make an effort to

TIME IS PRECIOUS TO WOMEN

➤ *63% of working women spend 40 hours or more on the job.*

➤ *40% of women 25 to 54 years old report that they have less than one hour a day for themselves.*

A HAPPY ENDING

Even women who buy a car online in order to save money and avoid the hard sell eventually have to visit the dealership, if only to sign papers and take delivery.

Said one woman with relief, "The salesman assigned to me obviously wanted to make sure I got exactly what I wanted. He directed all his remarks to me, not my husband. He is now on my list of great salespeople."

THE ULTIMATE SACRIFICE?

Letting the woman set the pace of the conversation is the equivalent of giving her the remote control.

be on time. If you are late for a good reason, apologize immediately and sincerely.

➤ *Let her set the pace each step of the way.* When you check with the woman before proceeding to the next step, you're showing respect by putting her in charge of the conversation.

Make a conscious effort to say things that put the woman in charge, such as "Is that something you'd like to get into today?" or "When you're ready, I'll be happy to go over that with you."

Avoid phrases like, "In order to save time, I'd like to...," "You need to make a decision now so you don't lose the car," or "Let's move on to the next point." And never look at your watch, unless it's to hurry yourself along.

Instead of saying "I hate to rush you, but I have another appointment," put the onus on yourself: "It looks like I haven't scheduled enough time for our meeting. Would you like to set up another one?"

➤ *Use your manners.* It's very simple: a lack of courtesy is a dealbreaker with women. So dust off your manners, and remember that women will also notice how you treat other people. One woman reported that although the service manager was very nice to *her,* he didn't treat the mechanics who worked for him very well. "Sure, he was polite to me, because I was the customer," she said, "but I could see that he really wasn't a very nice person."

Because a woman may be more sensitive to being snubbed or excluded, avoid humor or topics of conversation she doesn't care about or is offended by.

Wait to use nicknames until she invites you to. You don't want to run the risk of seeming pushy. In this regard, you'll probably want to ask rather than assume that your relationship is on a first-name basis.

3. *Understand her on her own terms.*

For a woman, the goal of a conversation is to understand and to be understood as a person, not just in business terms. The point is not simply to trade information or establish dominance, as it often is for men.

As the D-gene tells us, women's natural ways of speaking and listening are different from men's. Women tend to avoid black-or-white statements. They use more qualifiers and disclaimers, in an effort to invite the other person into the conversation. Women also ask more questions and use upward vocal inflections in order to check whether the other person is in step with them.

Little girls expect to take turns on the swing set and grown women expect the same thing when they talk. They hate having to fight to be heard. At times, a woman may appear hesitant or timid in conversation. In fact, her pauses are quite functional. She's put her foot on the conversational brake and is telling you it's your turn to proceed. But don't hog the road, because she expects you to do the same—give her back the right of way in a minute or so.

WHAT THIS MEANS FOR YOU

If you can modify your own conversational style to get in sync with your women customers, you'll be letting them know that you take them seriously and are tracking with them on both a business and interpersonal level. If you can enter their world by being respectful of—and responsive to—their preferred conversational style, you'll get insights you could never otherwise hope for into their needs and decision-making rationales. For a sales professional who wants to establish a long-term business relationship, this is critical information.

HOW TO BRIDGE THE D-GENE

Don't be surprised if this principle proves challenging. Women's and men's conversational styles and the dynamics of their inter-actions are very different. Men listen differently than women. They react much less. The first time we gave a presentation to an all-male audience, we thought we were bombing. They just sat there. Afterward, they had lots of questions and comments. It became obvious that they had been listening closely, but it hadn't looked that way to us during the presentation. When we speak to groups of women, on the other hand, it can feel as if the building is about to take off. They smile, they nod, they gesture, they make comments to their friends. It's... well, it's different.

> ➤ *Value her conversation style.* Expect it to be more detailed and descriptive than what you will hear from men. If you can stop trying to net out what she's saying, or get her to cut to the chase, you'll learn a lot about who she is. And what sales person doesn't need to know more about his or her customers?

> ➤ *Over-respond!* If women don't get frequent responses, they will assume you're not listening. So over-respond. It may feel forced at first, but you'll get used to it, and she'll get the picture that you're paying attention. By over-responding we mean nodding, maintaining eye contact, dropping in some "uh-huhs" and "I sees," and asking questions to learn more Say things like: "What was that like for you?", and reflecting back her feelings: "You

sound angry. I'd feel the same way if I were in your position." We'll have more to say on this topic in Chapter 6.

➤ *Pay attention.* It bears repeating that a woman hates talking to a man who is pretending to listen. You think women don't know that blank look when they see it? Think again. If you want to establish trusting relationships with your women customers, you need to come up with some tuning-in strategies. One salesman confessed that he pretends he is in math class and he's going to be quizzed on everything his customer is telling him.

➤ *Resist the temptation to interrupt.* We said it before and we'll say it again: DON'T INTERRUPT! Women will think you're rude. They will think you're not taking them seriously. It also makes a woman angry to be cut off when she's about to give you information that's important to her. And to top it all off, her anxiety rises because she feels she must compete to be heard.

Remember the woman who bought the minivan *and* the convertible? Would the salesperson have made the sale if he had cut her off before he learned of her passion for convertibles? You're cutting yourself short by cutting her off from saying things that could be useful to you. Interrupting is a huge mistake.

4. *Surpass her every expectation.*

Although men certainly appreciate service above and beyond the call of duty, by and large your efforts to exceed expectations will have an even bigger impact on women. It makes them feel special, it tells them you value the relationship, and it gives them the comfortable feeling that they are being well taken care of. Finally, there's no better way to set yourself apart from—and above—your competition.

There are two parts to making this principle work for you. First, provide her with extra help to make sure transactions go as smoothly as possible for her. Second, make thoughtful gestures that underscore the importance of the relationship to you.

WHAT THIS MEANS FOR YOU

Women have exceptional memories, and they like to share with other people. If you are able to do more for them than you promised and provide them with small extras even before they can think to ask for them, they'll reward you with their business, and also recommend you to their friends.

HOW TO BRIDGE THE D-GENE

The dual challenge for most salespeople is to remember how important going the extra mile is for their women customers, and to be as creative as possible in doing it. It's not about sending flowers or making the grand gesture. It's about knowing enough about her to do just the thing that will make her life a little happier and more hassle-free. In other words, this is where all that listening you've been doing can really pay off.

> **IT WORKS BOTH WAYS**
>
> *Historically, women have pushed for more and better service—like stores staying open 24/7, for example. Once in place, however, these improvements appealed as much to men as they did to women.*

A car salesman knew that one of his customers lived in a subdivision close to his. She was a young mother with three kids and a stressful job. He offered to switch cars with her on the days hers needed service. He would pick up her car the night before her service appointment and return it at the end of the day. During the day, she had his van to use. When returning her car one time, she commented on how much easier it was for her to get the kids and their car seats in and out of the van. Later in the week, a customer traded in a minivan on a newer model. The salesperson ran some numbers and called his customer. He took her car in trade and sold her the minivan. He delivered the van and the papers for her to sign. He switched license plates. She never set foot in the showroom. Since the car and the minivan, he has sold her two more vans and sold her husband a truck and a car. He has also sold cars to her mother, her hairdresser, her coworker, and the minister at her church.

➤ *Attend to the details.* Making an effort to become more detailed-oriented can really pay off. If you call a customer to make an appointment, and you're able to say, "I know you work late Thursday. How about Friday?" She'll appreciate the fact that you remembered her schedule.

If you have a hard time remembering your own wedding anniversary, you may want to think about getting some help. Is there someone in your office who can make sure you keep track of things? Would your dealer principal be willing to buy a software program to help track customer data?

➤ *Under-promise and over-deliver.* It's always safer to take the conservative path. In the first place, a woman doesn't like people who toot their own horns, and if you make outlandish promises, that's what she'll think you're doing. Second, when you can't deliver, you not only disappoint her, you add seeds of doubt about just how important she is to you, and how trustworthy you are overall. So if the SUV won't come in for two weeks, tell her that, and then do whatever you can to get it there faster.

IT PAYS TO BE A FRIEND

The best salespeople think of themselves as friends of their customers. The help they offer does not always have a lot to do with selling cars.

Murphy has been selling the Raftons new cars for years. Because of his connections with car repair, he's also been able to help three of their children get summer jobs. To him, whatever help he can give is part and parcel of his job.

➤ *Do everything you can to make her life easier.* If something has gone wrong for her, step in, and fix it. If the screw-up is somewhere in your own organization, find out who's responsible. Follow up, and let her know what you're doing. (We'll have more to say about this in Chapter 9.)

➤ *Surprise her with unexpected human gestures.* How about always having some special cookies for your customers to go with the free soft drinks the dealership offers? Tell her you love Thin Mints and to call when her daughter's Brownie troop is selling them—then buy a dozen packages! Or send her a newspaper clipping that relates to something she told you. Little acts of thoughtfulness tell her she's important enough for you to have listened—and remembered. When you send a greeting card or follow-up note, do you use dealership stationery, or do you take the trouble to pick out a nice card you think she would like? (We'll explore this topic in greater detail in Chapter 10.)

5. *Telegraph confidence.*

A woman wants a qualified and reliable ally in the sales process, someone who projects both confidence and competence. If you come across as anything less than capable and trustworthy, women customers will pick it up. For this reason, it's important to be fully aware of the verbal and nonverbal messages you send.

WHAT THIS MEANS FOR YOU

When everything about you conveys a sense of confidence that is genuine and compelling, women customers react by placing their trust in you.

HOW TO BRIDGE THE D-GENE

The biggest challenge for sale professionals—for everyone, really—is to feel confident so you can project confidence. On the other hand, you can feel confident and still send out messages that women will interpret differently, especially when they first meet you.

➤ *Develop a deep reservoir of product knowledge.* Increased product knowledge breeds self-confidence. If you get into situations where you feel as if you're winging it, go back and do some more homework. Remember, the point is not to overwhelm your customer with details, but to develop enough product knowledge to feel confident you can handle any situation. Your confidence is what she's looking for.

> **STUDY UP**
>
> *Because so much information is available on the Internet you need to know almost as much about your competitors' cars and trucks as about your own. Customers will have seen comparisons of safety and performance, and will have pointed questions for you.*

A woman we know tells of going to a Honda dealership to buy a CR-V. She had done her research and learned that there was a recall on the vehicle because of the possibility of engine fires. She mentioned it to a salesperson. He brushed it off with a terse, "Never heard of it." She went to another dealership. There the salesperson told he hadn't heard that but he'd check. Then and there, he called the service department manager and found out she was right, there was a recall and they had already taken care of the repair on all of their in-stock vehicles. Then and there, she bought the car.

➤ *Smile.* A smile is one of a sales person's most under-used tools. There's no more powerful way to let your customers know you're at ease and feeling good about what you're doing.

➤ *Behave confidently.* Did you know research shows that if you behave confidently, you'll eventually come to feel more confident? This is known in some circles as the "fake it 'til you make it" rule. Your mother had it right when she told you to stand up straight, don't slouch, develop a firm (not bone-crushing) handshake, look the other person in the eye and don't mumble. She should also have told you to speak clearly with an upbeat tone in your voice. You might want to call her and tell her that a lot of solid research confirms her advice.

While you need to put these principles into play whenever you work with women, they are absolutely essential during what we call the Two-Minute Takeoff. That comes next.

5 THE TWO-MINUTE TAKEOFF

Firing on All Five Principles

Let's take a moment to review where we are. You've learned about just how big the women's market is for cars and trucks. You've learned about the D-gene—how men and women are different, and why an understanding of the difference matters to your success. We've talked about five principles that will help you build trust. And you've learned that if she doesn't trust you, you're toast.

OK. You've absorbed all that, in a cerebral sort of way, and are about to have a conversation with a customer of the female persuasion. She's driven onto the lot. She's entered the showroom. You're up. What do you do next?

Maybe you should wing it. After all, you're a professional. You no doubt have a lot of experience working with customers. However, what if someone told you that within the first two minutes of meeting you, a woman will decide whether or not you are someone she can do business with? Would it make you step back and reconsider your approach?

Most customers, both male and female, approach the lease or purchase of a vehicle with some degree of trepidation, and if you're an experienced auto sales professional, you know why. After all, a car represents a big chunk of change for most people, and, unlike many other purchases, the final price is not fixed, but negotiated by you and your customer. They know you negotiate these deals every day of your life. A customer, on average, buys a car every three to four years. It shouldn't surprise you, then, that many customers walk into a dealership with their defenses up. You may even have been told that this is good—use the customer's defensiveness to negotiate a better deal for you!

If this is true for men, it's doubly true for women. When a woman meets you for the first time, she may already have some half-conscious preconceptions about you, based on her prior experiences with other people in sales. You know what they are, right? She thinks you won't take her seriously. She thinks you'll take advantage of her relative lack of experience. And if you're a man, you might even make a pass.

Not fair, you say? You're not that kind of person. You're right, it isn't fair, but that's the way life is sometimes.

Your first task is not to take this personally. These preconceptions are not about you, specifically. You may be the most D-gene-savvy person on the planet, but since you are someone who sells for a living, you come with a certain amount of baggage. And—we'll say it clearly—if you are male, your load of baggage could be sizeable.

Does this mean she's a raging feminist? Absolutely not. Does she have a chip on her shoulder? Not at all. Let's just say that she's got a lifetime of experience that tells her to be alert to any signs that she's not being taken seriously.

If you are a female sales associate, does any of this apply? Not in any gender-related way, of course, but the underlying anxiety and distrust may still be there. Read on to find out more.

Obviously you'll want to make sure you are observing each of the five principles of trust-based selling in your first meeting. The old adage says you'll never get a second chance to make a great first impression. So, we've put together the *Maddox Smye Never-Fail Steps to a Successful Two-Minute Takeoff*. Very short and sweet. Ready?

Step 1. Go to her. Don't make her come to you.

Why? Think back to when you were in high school and you had to walk across the gym floor to ask a girl or a guy to dance. How did you feel? Exposed? Vulnerable? Unsure of yourself? She's feeling a little like that when she enters the showroom. It's up to you to create a safe environment in which she can open up and start sharing the reason for her visit. The safer and more comfortable she feels, the easier it will be for you to create the kind of relationship she's looking for—one that will result in a sale.

Step 2. Shake her hand.

Women are touchier, in the sense of liking to touch, than men. On the other hand, any touching between the sexes in the workplace these days is generally a bad idea, especially if it's initiated by a man. A handshake is the exception. So take the initiative. Don't wait for her to offer her hand; in the business world we've gone beyond that bit of Victorian etiquette. This is all about extending yourself, so extend your hand and shake hers firmly. If you're a man, shake her hand in much the way you would shake a man's hand, remembering, of course, that your hand is probably bigger than hers and your grip may be stronger.

> **BUT WHAT IF SHE DOESN'T FEEL THIS WAY?**
>
> *Act as if she does, and you can't go wrong.*
>
> *First of all, she probably does feel this way to some extent—even if she's very successful in her own field, and even if she seems totally in charge.*
>
> *Besides, these behaviors are all common sense. They just happen to be more important to women than to men.*

Step 3. Introduce yourself—slowly.

You probably already know that whenever people approach a major purchase, their anxiety level goes up—sometimes way up. Anxious people can't listen very well. As a finance manager in a southern dealership said, "People hear what they want to hear sometimes. You have to repeat what you say, write it down. Otherwise you'll be misunderstood."

So take your time when you tell her your name, especially if it's a mouthful. Give her a card so she can read it. Names are often easier to understand when people can see them.

Step 4. Maintain eye contact and SMILE.

Women make and maintain eye contact more than men. That's part of the D-gene, as you learned in Chapter 3. Watch a man who is introduced to someone, male or female. Very shortly after meeting, his eyes will begin to shift—to other people in the room, to a picture on the wall, to his shoes, to nothing much at all. To a woman, this behavior literally looks shifty, and makes her wonder what he's really thinking. Some people have a hard time making and sustaining eye contact. This is one time when you need to suck-it-up and just do it! There is an old actor's trick that says to focus on one eye, or pick a spot between the other person's eyes and concentrate on that. We think a better approach is to look directly at the person's eyes, but don't maintain eye contact too long. Keep it at 10-15 seconds or the time it takes you to speak a sentence.

Don't forget to smile. When you smile upon first meeting a customer, you're conveying a lot: I'm happy to meet you, I like what I'm doing, I feel confident that I can help you and that we will work well together. You probably can't fake a smile—not one you'd want anybody to see—but you can try to have the kinds of positive, upbeat feelings that will make you feel like smiling. So make the effort to put yourself in a positive mood: a genuine smile is hard to resist and it's contagious.

Step 5. Offer refreshments.

Research shows that the more senses you can engage, the stronger the connection you can create. What creates a stronger connection than sharing food or a beverage?

If she's come to your dealership, stale office coffee won't impress her. How about some special blend, a selection of exotic teas, a soft drink, or a bottle of water? And while we're on the subject, do you have some halfway decent cups and saucers? Nice paper napkins? Fresh cookies? Candies? Get things set up now, and you'll be ready when she arrives.

And while you're setting up the food, look around. Is your dealership clean and bright? Does it ooze *warm and friendly*, or is it cold and sterile? How does it smell—like grease and oil, or freshly baked cookies? Do you have a safe place for children to play—or will they run the Matchbox cars on the side of an SUV? Do you have coloring books and crayons in your desk drawer? What else will make her feel instantly welcome?

That's it. Five simple steps to a great Two-Minute Takeoff. We told you it wouldn't take long.

Now you're ready to move into the sales conversation itself.

MASTERING THE ART OF FEMALE-FOCUSED LISTENING

How to Uncover Her Unique Needs and Wants

"You're not listening!"

If the average man pocketed a nickel for each time he got this complaint from a woman, his pants would fall down.

Let's face it, guys, you are notorious for not listening to women. Even women customers. You know you're supposed to—they're customers, after all—but still you find yourself tuning out. Why? If you're being honest, you'll probably admit to one or more of these reasons:

➤ I know in 15 seconds what she needs.

➤ I've heard it all before.

➤ I've heard it all before *from* her.

➤ I know what she means.

➤ I know what she's trying to say.

➤ Most of what she's saying is irrelevant.

> **HUSBAND'S NOTE TO HIS WIFE**
>
> *Someone from the Guyna Colleges called.*
>
> *They said the Pabst Beer is normal.*
>
> *I didn't know you liked beer.*

No wonder one of the first questions men ask in our workshops is not, "How can I learn to listen better?" but "How can I get her to shut up?"

These men certainly don't like our answer, which is, "You can't"—until they realize how they can turn this initial part of the sales process into the beginning of a profitable buying and selling partnership.

So, let's assume you've successfully achieved a Two-Minute Takeoff with a woman customer. What's your next move? Choose one of the following:

A. Lock in her initial interest by making sure she knows your stellar qualities as a salesman who is D-gene-certified.

B. Ask her what she's looking for.

C. Ask how you can help her make the best use of her time.

You probably said "C," because you figured the correct answer to multiple-choice questions like these is usually the last choice. You're right, but do you know *why?*

> **"HELP" OR "HELPFUL"?**
>
> *Do you know why "How can I be most helpful to you today?" is a better question than "How can I help you today?"*
>
> *Because the first question focuses on how you can serve her, while the second implies that she's weak and needs help.*
>
> *Small point? Maybe, but small points add up.*

The answer goes back to the second principle of trust-based selling: Respect her, her time, and her timing. By asking her how you can make the best use of her time, you're showing respect for the fact that she probably has every minute of her day accounted for, and you want to make sure you don't take too much of her time.

People who sell cars usually have a series of questions they like to ask new customers: What are you looking for? What are you driving now? What do you like/not like about it? Your female customer is perfectly capable of answering them. But here's where you have to be careful. If you make it sound like you're going down a list, the D-gene antenna will be activated and she will wonder if you're

> **WHAT SHE'S LOOKING FOR**
>
> *Are you "merely" doing a good job, or do you really care about what she's telling you?*

really listening to her or just filling in the blanks on some verbal check list. She will become a little anxious. Are you really getting her situation? Do you understand the dynamics of her life enough to make the kinds of recommendations that will suit her best?

In other words, women aren't very happy with only yes-or-no short-answer questions. They want you to understand their lives, not because they think they're so fascinating, but because this is the kind of information they'd want if they were in your position.

That's at the level of information. At another level, sharing information is part of a woman's way of building a relationship. She's telling you about her family, or her work, or her goals and concerns, as a way of establishing common ground. As one saleswoman with a lot of women customers put it, "When you work with a woman, you establish a relationship not just with her but with everyone and everything in her life that she takes care of, worries about, or feels responsible for."

FEELING FINDER

One sales professional we spoke to said she created a "feeling finder" form to elicit a customer's priorities, concerns, and future security issues.

Meanwhile, of course, your clock is ticking. The mantra "time is money" is going through your head. You have appointments. You have sales goals. As she talks, you may find yourself getting antsy and your attention starting to wander. How long is this going to take? Is she a serious buyer or a tire-kicker? Did the Lakers win last night?

Fair enough. You've got your agenda and she's got hers. The thing is, she is the customer. Here's what we're saying: If you can find a way to tune in to her—*her* way—you'll be well rewarded.

SLOW DOWN

You're not barreling down the Interstate. You're touring the local roads—and learning a great deal about your customer as you go.

In this chapter, we're going to tell you four things you can do to uncover her unique needs and wants in a female-focused way. Before we get started, however, you need to let go of any previous plans or preconceptions you may have had about the meeting's outcome. Think of what you're doing in this conversation as beginning a process, not working towards a specific outcome. The more you discuss her life situation, the more she may realize that she has multiple needs that exceed the immediate reason for contacting you. Remember the woman who came in for a minivan and drove out with the minivan *and* a convertible?

Taking the time to get to know her and her expectations helps establish your credibility. It shows her that you value her and the relationship as much as you do a sale, and gives her the confidence of knowing that your recommendations will suit her special needs and circumstances.

TAP INTO HER STORY

If customers distrust car salespeople, salespeople have their reasons for not always taking customers at face value—for thinking, in fact, that "buyers are liars." Unlike, say, a stock broker or an insurance salesman, the salesman on the showroom floor faces a much broader spectrum of customers who walk in the door, claiming (or pretending) that they want to buy a car. The trick is separating the serious buyers from those who want to get out of the heat and kill an afternoon.

To make sense out of all this variety, it's tempting for salespeople to categorize customers in terms of certain stereotypes simply by their appearance and the kind of car they drive onto the lot: the little old lady, the midlife crisis guy, the soccer mom, the business executive. A whole set of terms has evolved among car salespeople to label a customer's buying behaviors: the be-back, the mooch, the grinder, the lay down. Having tagged his prospect with one of these labels, the salesperson can then turn off his mind and sell to the stereotype instead of the real customer.

The manager of a luxury car dealership in Texas makes this point with a story about something that happened to him:

"Early in my career I was selling European sports cars. One day a nice-looking older lady maybe in her 70's and a younger man

drove up in this big old two-door Cadillac. They wanted to drive one of my cars. At first I thought the man was the customer, but the woman turned out to be the buyer. Maybe because she reminded me of my grandmother, or maybe because of the car she was driving, I recommended several lighter, entry-level models with automatic transmissions. She drove two or three, and said she liked them, but it was obvious she wasn't thrilled.

On the way back to the showroom she saw one of our top-of-the-line models all the way across the lot—powerful engine, manual transmission, practically a racing car, and it was fire-engine red. Her eyes lit up and she asked if she could take it out. I agreed, after I managed to stop myself from telling her it was way too much car for a woman. Of course, that was the car she fell in love with.

After we had agreed on a price, she opened up and said that her husband had recently died, and she was looking for a car that would get her out of her normal routine and make her feel young again. Her husband was very conservative but had left her a lot of money (that was his car they drove up in), price was no object, and she really wanted that red car.

That experience taught me that if I wanted to be successful, I had to set aside whatever initial assumptions I might make about a customer, and learn as much about them as I could."

This story builds on something a dealer in New Jersey told us. "Some women are so concerned about making a good deal that they start out playing their cards very close to the chest," he said. "If you don't draw them out, they won't reveal much of anything. Then, once you make a deal, they relax and open up. That's when you get a lot of information that would have been helpful to have earlier in the transaction."

You no doubt already know the kinds of questions that will encourage her to share:

➤ How can I make the best use of your time right now?

➤ What are your priorities in a car? What do you need a new vehicle for?

➤ What did you like about your old vehicle? What didn't you like?

➤ What do you want in your new vehicle?

She may not have sound-bite answers to all these questions. She may instead do what most of us do, men as well as women, which is to use the process of answering to think through what she means, adding layers of context as she talks. You can strengthen your connection with her by creating a judgment-free zone in which she can think through her needs, asking for your advice when she needs it.

STAY TUNED INTO HER

You don't simply need to pay attention. You need to show her that you're paying attention.

This is another one of those D-gene moments. Men and women behave differently when they're listening. Men may not make eye contact. They may look distracted, or stare out the window, or appear lost in thought. They may have a frown on their faces. None of this means they're not listening. Quite the contrary, they may be concentrating deeply.

When women are listening, on the other hand, they don't just sit there. They make eye contact. They nod. They *respond.* They react *physically.* They share their own experiences in an effort to draw the other person closer. All this, to a woman, is listening. What a man does is… something else, she's not quite sure what. Since she's already anxious about not being taken seriously, it's easy for her to leap to conclusions when she sees you just sitting there. Maybe you're bored, she thinks. Maybe you think she's stupid. Maybe you're just waiting to contradict her.

Your challenge, therefore, is to pay attention *visibly*.

Show her you're listening. Demonstrate your interest through eye contact, head nods, voice tone, and short phrases.

Listen with your eyes as well as your ears. What message are her body language and facial expressions giving you? Is it different from what she's saying? If you catch something that you don't understand, or if her words and body language don't match, ask her to clarify. Say something like:

"You said you wanted a low-mileage car, but you also really seemed to respond to all the flexibility of the four-wheel drive."

ASK HER QUESTIONS TO CLARIFY MEANING, FEELINGS, AND DETAILS

Once she's answered your broad questions, you'll need to sift and sort through what she's told you in order to tailor the solution that's best for her. The more you can link your questions back to something specific she said, or to an emotional state, the more she'll realize that you were really listening. Here are some clarifying questions you can ask:

"You said you need to do something right away. What's your time frame?"

"What was it that made your prior service experience so frustrating for you?"

"When you say "safety," what does that mean to you?"

> **SAFETY OR PERFORMANCE?**
>
> Women like safety in a car, but they also like performance. Many, in fact, will consider power to be a safety feature, in that it helps them safely access fast-moving lanes of traffic on freeways.

Make sure your questions reflect your need for clarification or for more information, rather than any suggestion that she's not expressing herself clearly. Since women tend to be self-deprecating, you need to go out of your way not to give this impression.

Make it as easy as possible for her to provide information. Try to keep the exchange conversational, so she never feels as if you're putting her on the spot.

CONVEY YOUR UNDERSTANDING SO SHE KNOWS SHE'S BEEN HEARD

Women want to know they've been correctly understood. They want to make sure you got the facts, but they also want to know you understand the important nuances of their situation. So at key points in your discussion, play back your understanding of the facts and how she feels about them.

"You want to make sure you have the money left to have your old car checked out and repaired so you'll feel secure about your daughter driving it. Do I have that right?"

You need to make sure your understanding is accurate, because it will become the basis of the subsequent work you do with her.

Don't be surprised if you don't get it right the first time. She may have given you a great deal of big-picture information to process, and it may take you some time to extract the meaning she intended. Don't let this bother you. This kind of collaborative process is embedded in the D-gene. Besides, there are benefits of not getting it right the first time:

➤ She gets to explain some more, which translates into more bonding.

➤ She gets to correct you, which if it doesn't happen too often, will make you seem more human to her. Besides, what woman doesn't like to correct a man?

By the same token, she may well change her mind when she hears your summary. What's important is not what she told you but the understanding you eventually arrive at together.

How well have you been listening to your women customers?

According to recent surveys by the *Detroit Free Press* and others, here are some features women have been asking for in their cars. Is this what you're hearing from your customers?

> ➤ *Fuel efficiency.*
> ➤ *Quality.* They want trouble-free vehicles and fewer trips to the service department.
> ➤ *Safety.* They want seat belts, air bags, stability control, and crash ratings, as well as special anchors for child seats.
> ➤ *Maintenance.* They want it to be convenient and infrequent.
> ➤ *Comfort.* They want vehicles that accommodate differences in men's and women's strength and stature, and ease of getting in and getting out.
> ➤ *Thoughtful details.* They want compartments and hooks to hold purses, lighted mirrors, and spring-assisted, nail-friendly door and hatchback openers.
> ➤ *Storage.* They want lots of it, and they want it to be stylish.
> ➤ *Cleanliness.* They want nonpolluting vehicles with interiors that are easy to clean.
> ➤ *Style.* They appreciate it.
> ➤ *Value.* They want to pay a fair price for what they get.

Pitfalls

1. *Don't short-circuit the process by telling her what she wants.* You may be right. After all, this is your job, and you speak to customers every day. Even so, you're robbing the customer of the ability to crystallize her thoughts and share them with you. You're also neglecting the

relationship-building that happens when she tells you her story.

2. *Don't pepper her with questions.* You're not a traffic cop, and she's not a speeder. Avoid series of closed questions, especially those that call for a yes or no answer. After you ask a question, give her plenty of time to answer. Add your reactions to what she has said before jumping in with the next question.

3. *Avoid leading questions.* Women are especially sensitive to questions that seem designed to manipulate or patronize. "You want to save money, don't you?" or statements beginning "I'm sure you'd agree that..." fall into this category.

4. *Keep your distance.* Avoid leaning into her personal space, making her feel threatened. Women's personal space is larger than men's. Staying about an arm's length away from her is usually comfortable.

5. *Don't interrupt.* If you think we're repeating ourselves on this topic, it's because we are.

6. *Don't be afraid of silence.* Okay, you don't want to just sit there until she says something. After all, you're not a psychoanalyst. Still, a few gentle silences will have the effect of encouraging her to open up, especially if you then respond with nods and phrases of understanding.

The Next Phase

If everything has been going well, you've reached a common understanding about what your customer wants. You and she have begun to feel more comfortable with each other as you have shown your respect for her and interest in her as a person rather than just a customer. Now you're ready to move on to the next phase in the process, which is offering recommendations that you think will best meet her needs for a car or truck—and giving her the opportunity to see, touch, smell, and drive vehicles that you think will meet her needs.

But don't rush her. She'll let you know when she's ready. At this point, you need to move from a fairly free-wheeling conversation to a discussion of solutions, products, services, and recommendations. Your challenge will be to make this shift without leaving behind the conversational, collaborative tone you have worked hard to establish.

7 TURNING YOUR PRESENTATION INTO A CONVERSATION

How to Share the Information She Wants, the Way She Wants It

One of the things we love most about good sales professionals is their enthusiasm for the product or service they're selling. It's a pleasure to deal with people who are passionate about their work, and convinced that what they are selling is exactly what you need. Can you imagine making a major purchase from someone who lacks this quality?

Probably not. However...

Early on in the selling process, your customers—and especially your women customers—aren't ready for any heavy-duty selling. While women appreciate your passion, they're not ready for the close. You've built a relationship, and now it's time for you to share information, but not just any information. She doesn't want a mind-dump of everything you know. She wants information that applies specifically to her concerns, based on what you learned about her in the conversation the two of you have just had.

If you move too quickly, women are likely to think they're being hustled. Of course, men don't like to be hustled either, but they are usually able to dismiss it as part of the selling game. A woman, on the other hand, tends to take it personally. She won-

> **SEE, TOUCH, SMELL, TEST-DRIVE**
>
> *Says one sales manager, "When my salespeople complain about people not trusting them and the Internet making so much inside information available, I ask them, 'In how many other businesses can customers get their hands on a product and fall in love with it so quickly? How often do you think a car sells itself?'"*

ders if you really think she's stupid enough to buy the line of bull you're pushing. If women think they're being hustled, they're likely to leave and never come back.

So, if your normal procedure is to give a canned presentation to your customer, and this customer is a woman, you might want to rethink your game plan. Instead, your challenge is to maintain the conversational approach that you adopted when you were asking her about her needs, and still give her the information and/or recommendations that will help her make a decision.

CANNED PRESENTATIONS? WHO? ME?

The ability to shift seamlessly from asking about her needs to offering information or making recommendations about your product is the hallmark of trusted advisers. It's a natural shift for them because they don't have the "now it's time to sell her a car" mind-set. They see the whole experience in terms of constantly refining their knowledge of the customer. First they find out about her needs, and then they figure out how best to match their products with those needs.

Even though you may not make what you think of as a canned presentation, as an experienced sales professional you probably have certain approaches and patterns of speech— phrases or even whole paragraphs—that you have found effective when talking with customers about your products and services. Since in all probability most of your customers have been men, you may want to reexamine some of these "sure-fire" lines and techniques in light of how effective they are with women.

Here's a quick quiz to help you conduct an inventory:

	YES	NO
1. I use a lot of sports and military analogies.		
2. I typically present information for three minutes or more without interruption.		
3. I focus more on features than on benefits.		
4. I add value by making strong recommendations, since I'm more aware of the consequences of these decisions than most of my customers.		
5. Although I don't make canned presentations, I do rely on a few key phrases to explain my product or service.		
6. To move customers along, I sometimes use phrases like "you'll never go wrong…," "this opportunity won't last forever…" and "you can trust me when I tell you…"		
7. I use a lot of humor to make my points.		
8. I use phrases like "If you're like most people…"		
9. I describe benefits in terms of increased status, e.g., "this will help you really stand out from the crowd."		
10. I use a lot of directive terms: "you should," "you'll have to," and "you need to."		

None of these approaches is D-gene-friendly, with the possible exception of humor. We include it here because the particular humor that has proven effective with male customers might not necessarily work well with women. Have you ever watched men and women watching *The Three Stooges* or *South Park*? The guys are rolling on the floor, and the women are rolling their eyes. So be careful with humor.

People in our training seminars frequently ask us about prepared presentations aimed at women. If a standard version works with men, they want to know, why couldn't someone put together a presentation that was D-gene-friendly?

First of all, we question whether prepared presentations are as effective with men as many sales professionals think. Leaving that aside, just as we've never seen a workable standard screening set of questions, we've never come across a scripted presentation that works terribly well with woman customers. One reason is that a women has many questions that can take the presenter too far afield for a single script to be of much help. A bigger reason, however, is that a woman is looking for a unique solution that responds specifically to what she has told you; the slightest whiff of something canned will cause her to question just how much you really understand her situation.

So if you can't use your salesman shtick, what's left? Four skills that will enable you to give her the information she wants without undercutting your role as a trusted adviser.

MAKE IT A TWO-WAY STREET

Men, you'll remember, talk in longer chunks of time than women do. Women talk in shorter chunks, and they also take turns, pausing to give the other person a chance to step in. True, at this point you may have more to tell her than she has to tell you, although if you haven't done a good job of listening, you may not. So what do you do?

First, ask her what information she wants and the best way for you to provide it. The idea is to make sure she stays in charge of the process at all times. The following comparison illustrates the difference between telling her what she needs to know and putting her in the driver's seat.

GENERIC APPROACH	D-GENE-FRIENDLY APPROACH
It's a really solid safe automobile I'd recommend it to anybody.	What would you like to know about this model?
Remind me before you leave to give you a packet of information about the car.	Would you like a couple of articles to read?
There are basically three things you need to know about SUVs.	What about SUVs would you like more information on?

Of course, you'll still need to make sure that she gets all the information she needs to make an informed decision.

"Which features would you say are most important from your perspective?"

What we're talking about here is a matter of emphasis. Start with what she wants to know, instead of what you want her to know.

Answer her questions when she asks them, not when you would like to answer them. If you're one of those methodical people who eat all your peas and then all your mashed potatoes, even the thought of following this guideline could drive you crazy. All we're saying is, the more you can do to get on your customer's wavelength, the greater your chances of increasing your immediate sale, and the potential for additional sales down the road. It's your choice.

Give brief, concise answers to her questions, and then ask her what else she'd like to know. You're the product expert, and it's tempting to take her question and run with it. Keep in mind, however, that while you may be the product expert, you're not the expert at knowing what

WHAT'S YOUR MENTAL IMAGE?

Instead of thinking of a presentation as giving a speech, imagine that you are an expert witness in a trial, being questioned by a friendly lawyer.

HOW TO PATRONIZE AND DISCOUNT A CUSTOMER

"What a great question! I'll get to it in just a minute."

she wants. As a general rule, you probably shouldn't talk for more than a minute or two without giving her an opportunity to respond.

Check in with her periodically to see if she's getting what she wants. You're not looking for a grade on your performance. You know she's on a tight schedule, and you want to make sure she's getting the information she needs to make a decision.

It's important to determine how she prefers to learn. Is it by reading? Listening? Seeing a visual? All of us have a preferred learning style, and we respond to those who communicate well with us. Women respond well to stories of people like themselves; stories that include descriptions of how the product you're selling has solved a problem for someone or improved her life.

Unlike many other sales professionals, you represent a product that can sell itself once a customer can see, touch, smell and drive it. This is true for your female as much as for your male customers—if you have established positive, trusting working customer relationships with them.

Until you know what kind of learner she is, try different approaches. Watch her face and see if she responds. If she seems uninterested in a factual explanation, you might say, "Here's another way to look at it," and put the information in story form.

TAKE WHAT YOU'VE LEARNED FROM HER AND USE IT

There's nothing more effective than linking back everything you say about the car or truck to something she told you. It's a good selling practice in general, but it's especially effective when used with women.

This is another place where all the careful listening you did will pay off, by enabling you to make close links between what the vehicle can do and what she has told you she wants:

"And if you do plan to get into real estate, this navigation system will help you locate properties easily, and look professional with your clients."

"This model will easily accommodate a bike rack for those weekend trips you've been dreaming about."

"With all your new job responsibilities, at least you won't have to keep track of when this car needs service. It will tell you."

Here are some things you can do to let her know you're basing your suggestions and recommendations on what she told you:

➤ Refer to any notes you took—it let's her know you really paid attention.

➤ Use her exact words or phrases whenever possible. It's a good way to demonstrate your respect.

➤ Underscore any outcomes she feels strongly about.
   "This model has had one of the best service records of any car in its class."

➤ If you're offering a range of suggestions, prioritize them based on what you've learned is important to her.

➤ Use technical terms that match her level of knowledge and understanding.

➤ Select visual support, sales and marketing materials she'll find relevant and useful to share with others.

➤ Paint word pictures that help make your point.
   "You can put all your equipment in this van and easily retrieve it at a client's site without a lot of shifting and lifting. You'll look cool, professional and very well-organized."

➤ Be enthusiastic about the solution you're recommending.

> **SIMPLIFY, SIMPLIFY**
>
> *Automotive technology has become very complex. Your challenge is to simplify the features, but without withholding information that will make the woman suspect you're hiding something.*

Of course, it goes without saying that customers also convey information about what they need less directly. If you've been tuning into your customer's body language and tone of voice as well as her words, you may have picked up some unspoken concerns or fears. It's probably more effective to acknowledge these indirectly. Avoid saying something like, "It seems to me this car may be too sporty and fast for you." Instead, ask her what she thinks about the car she's just driven.

POSITION THE TOTAL CUSTOMER EXPERIENCE TO HER

If you want to distinguish yourself from your competition, you need to demonstrate to the customer how you yourself add value, separate from the vehicle you sell. One of the strongest differentiators, especially for women, is the service you and members of your team provide.

When it comes to developing a long-term relationship with a customer, especially a woman customer, service is HUGE. If you do it right, service is the thread that will link her to your dealership—getting her into the dealership on a regular basis, creating opportunities to discuss after-market products, and setting the stage for the purchase of her next car or truck. As one dealer put it, "Selling a customer her first car is the hard part. The second and third cars are easier—and you can often make more money on them, because she's willing to pay for the special treatment you give."

The salesperson we told you about earlier, who picked up his neighbor's car and brought it in to the shop for service, had this down pat. He knew how to shake himself loose from the crowded field of car salespeople.

Here are some other ways D-gene-savvy salespeople position the service experience with their women customers:

➤ At the end of her first visit to the showroom, even before she buys a car, the salesperson escorts her back to the service department so she can see what it looks like. He also describes how appointments are made, what will happen when she brings her car in, and answers any questions she might have.

➤ Once she has purchased the car but before she drives it off the lot, he takes her back to the service department, and introduces her to the service manager and/or a service writer, so she feels she has a personal connection with someone when she first brings her car in. They make an appointment for her first service visit at that time.

While introducing the customer to service people, he includes information about her that will help them remember her: "Mrs. Johnson has just bought a new XX7. She has three boys, sells insurance, and says she is always short on time. I told her you guys would never keep her waiting."

The D-gene-savvy service person remembers details, and builds on them with each succeeding visit.

➤ So that the woman doesn't feel the salesperson is dumping and running now that the sale is complete, he stresses the continuity of their relationship by encouraging her to contact him if she ever has a problem.

"Here's my cell phone number. Don't hesitate to use it if anything comes up where I can help you."

None of these steps will make a dime's worth of difference, however, if the dealership doesn't do its part. This means streamlining the process of making appointments, servicing vehicles,

WELCOME!

Unlike most service departments, which have a "No Customers Permitted Beyond this Point," one dealer put up a sign that says, "Welcome to Our Technology Center."

"We invite people to watch their cars being repaired," he says.

meeting all time commitments—and, above all, making sure the service department and its waiting areas—*and bathrooms*—are clean and attractive. While women customers may appreciate current magazines that include their interests and even facilities to access the Internet, nothing is as make-or-break as cleanliness.

> *"I pay a full-time porter just to make sure the floor of the service department is clean and shining, garbage cans are empty, and the restrooms are spotless," claims one dealer.[1] "We don't have any oil spots on the floor or spare parts lying around. Everyone who works there wears a uniform, and it's clean. 'Cleaner than my kitchen,' many women have told me."*

MAKE YOUR NETWORK HER NETWORK

One of your greatest assets is your roster of other satisfied customers. Consider them your fan club, and don't be afraid to call on them. If a woman customer has some concerns or objections, tell stories about satisfied customers who had similar concerns at first. Offer to put her in contact with some customers who would be willing to share their experiences. Giving her the chance to share her situation and learn from others is a very D-gene-friendly way to resolve concerns. It removes you from the expert role, and enables her to get a sense of the kind of person you are from other customers.

Pitfalls

Here are some behaviors to avoid when you're sharing information about your product or service:

➤ *Badmouthing the competition.* It's not a good idea under any circumstances, but women find it especially objec-

---

[1] Virgil Skinner, Southwest Infiniti Dealer

tionable. How can they be sure that you won't bad-mouth them behind their backs?

➤ *Bragging.* Women are very suspicious of overt bragging. But don't worry. If you make sure your plaques, certificates, and awards are prominently displayed in your office, these inanimate objects will do your bragging for you.

➤ *Talking down.* The trick here is to examine your assumptions. If you assume that women "can't understand figures" or "don't get technology," you need to update your thinking. Everyone learns and understands differently. One way is not better or worse than any other. We won't bore you with the women who have made fortunes understanding figures and "getting" technology. We could mention the woman who has built eBay into a multi-billion dollar corporation, but we won't. Just keep in mind that the more you can adapt to your customers' preferences, the greater your chances of increasing your sales.

➤ *Lecturing.* Don't use her question or comment to launch into a lecture. Keep it conversational. Remember, her head-nodding means that she hears you, not that she agrees with you. If she does too much nodding, you're doing too much talking.

➤ *Humor.* Guys banter and rib each other as a way to make contact. Many women don't like it, so don't do it.

➤ *Pressure tactics.* Men think they've won at the negotiating game when the salesperson chases them to the door offering to drop the price of the vehicle another $500 if he'll sign right now. Women, on the other hand, see that as a breach of trust. They think that if he can drop the price $500 that easily, he must be trying to cheat her. She won't be back.

8 MAKING THE SALE HER WAY

How to Complete a Pressure-less Close

Let's be frank. No matter how much effort you put into creating a trust-based relationship with a customer, the fact remains that as an auto sales professional you make your living closing deals. There is absolutely nothing wrong with that. The whole purpose of this book is to help you close more deals. The only problem is that the highly manipulative closing techniques sometimes associated with car sales ("What color should we order that in?"), don't work well with women. In fact, in this day and age of consumer awareness and easily accessible information, they don't work very well, period.

When it comes to closing, most salespeople know that customers don't like a hard sell, and they try not to appear too aggressive. If the customer is a woman, they may make an extra effort. Yet when they reach the point of wanting to close and the woman isn't ready, or doesn't seem ready, their good intentions can fly out the window, and they're suddenly all over her—pushing and pressuring her for a decision. The result? What had looked like a sure thing suddenly turns very, very cold.

A BE-BACK? OR JUST BUSY?

When women meet with a salesperson, they always go in with an exit strategy— I've got to pick up my son from soccer practice, or I'm meeting a friend in 30 minutes. That way, if the meeting doesn't go well, they can leave without a confrontation or hurt feelings. The problem for the salesperson is that he may have lost a customer without ever knowing why.

We recognize that closing a deal can be a stressful experience for you. You've invested time in the customer, and you want it—you need it—to pay off, and so does your manager. The greater the pressure you feel, the greater the temptation to shift your focus from serving the customer to making the sale, even though you know better. The thought that you might lose a sale puts you under stress, and during periods of stress it's normal to fall back on old behaviors even if you've come to see that those old techniques are not effective. It happens simply because they're familiar and you're under stress. That's why, as your focus on closing, you might be tempted to forget everything you've learned about the D-gene and default to high-pressure mode, forgetting that any pressure is a turn-off to a woman.

GROUND ZERO?

Many customers of both genders see the automobile showroom as Ground Zero for the high-pressure close. While customers ascribe this pressure solely to the salesperson, we realize what they may not—the pressure ultimately comes from the dealership's management and selling practices. Dealer principals have an inventory of cars sitting out the on the lot, costing them money. So they put pressure on the sales force: quotas, haranguing "motivational" talks, and the whiteboard that reveals to God and everybody exactly where you stand in relation to your colleagues. No wonder you feel pressure.

> *The beatings will continue...*
> *until morale improves.*
>
> —*written on a black T-shirt under a pirate's face*

And yet there are changes in the wind that are resulting in less pressure on the salesperson and therefore on the customer. Some dealerships are actually scrapping the commission structure and paying their salespeople a salary. This is often the case when the Internet has been involved in a sale. Because of the Internet, more and more customers arrive at a dealership much farther along in their buying process. They've researched the car they want, they have a good idea of a fair price, and in fact they are ready to buy. "The only thing that drives them away at this point," says one manager, "is a salesperson who gets cute with the price, or starts pushing for a bigger sale. If they knocked that stuff off, they could close in short order and be ready for the next sale."

A TRUE STORY

Mary Ann teaches third grade in a good school in an upscale Los Angeles suburb. She's married to a high school football coach. They enjoy all sports, and they both love surfing. The car Mary Ann has been driving has over 150,000 miles on it, and she's tired of tying of down the trunk lid and worrying that her board is going to fall out or be rammed from behind. She makes a decent salary and pays her bills on time. So, she's decided to bite the bullet and buy a truck big enough to haul both surfboards. One day, on the way home from school, she stops at the dealership she drives by every day and goes in to look. She's greeted by Sam, who is up for the next customer.

Now, let's see what he says and she says about the experience.

Sam's Version

Sam shook hands with Mary Ann, and liked her immediately. He recognized her as a straight-shooter and someone who wouldn't automatically assume he was trying to cheat her. He thought they developed a nice rapport. They were both interested in surfing. She had recently come back from Hawaii, where he was thinking about taking his next vacation. She had arrived with a lot of research about two light truck models she was interested in. She test-drove both, they discussed putting a rack on the roof for her surfboards, and negotiated a price they each could live with.

He was surprised, therefore, when she said she had to leave that evening to handle a business emergency, and wouldn't be able to finalize the sale until she returned. He pressed her to stay and complete the deal. He probed for what it would take to get her to buy the car now, fearing that if she left she would never come back. As a last resort he said he would consider lowering the price, but she was adamant about needing to return later to finish the sale.

At the end of their conversation he was having a hard time hiding his anger. All this time, he thought, and she splits. For a "business emergency." Right.

He called her a couple of times in the next few days, but she never called back. So much for their rapport. "It's true," he thought, "buyers are liars."

Mary Ann's Version

Mary Ann thought she had found in Sam someone she could trust. They had a lot in common and he seemed to really get what was important to her. That's why she was so surprised when, at the end, he poured on the pressure to buy. She had to be at her Mom's for the weekend, and she wanted to talk the truck purchase over with her husband, so she just didn't have time to finish the deal. But it was as if he didn't believe her when she said she'd come back. And what was the business of offering to lower the price? If he was willing to do that, maybe he was like all car salesmen, and she shouldn't have trusted him in the first place. Maybe she could take Sam's price and get a better deal somewhere else. She certainly wasn't going back to work with him.

What Went Wrong?

Sam did almost everything perfectly. But he blew it with the close. In his single-minded focus on closing the sale, he had forgotten that women hate to be pressured. Maybe his better judgment had been drowned out by the voice of his sales manager in his head—"What?! You let her go?! You really think she's coming back?" Bottom line? No sale for Sam. No truck for a disappointed Mary Ann, who has to begin the buying process all over again with another dealership.

Perhaps you are lucky enough to work for a dealership whose policies make it fairly easy for you to concentrate on the relationship rather than on the close. But even if you don't, you can create a pressure-less close if you keep in mind the five principles of trust-based selling we introduced in Chapter 3, "Not Until She Trusts You."

USING THE TRUST-BASED SELLING PRINCIPLES TO CLOSE

Like any new learning, these principles are easy to forget in moments of stress, so lets take another look at them now, and see how they can help you complete a pressure-less close.

1. Think relationship before product.

Remind yourself that women tend to be more loyal and less focused on "the deal" than men. Trust that the relationship you've developed so far will mean more to her than to a man. So, when she says she'll be back, chances are greater that she means what she says. This should reduce your anxiety level and help you remember that pushing her to do something she isn't ready for is a sure-fire way to make sure she doesn't return.

2. Respect her, her time, and her timing.

Acting on this principle is key during your efforts to close a sale. Women are often more sensitive to disrespect than men are, and there's nothing more disrespectful than trying to shoe-horn a customer into closing. Also, since most women are busier than most men, when she says she has to leave, doesn't have time, or wants input from her friends, it's not necessarily an excuse. Instead of pushing her to close on your schedule (or your sales manager's), ask her what you can do to make the process easier for her. She'll be grateful for your consideration.

3. Understand her on her own terms.

Closing a sale is no excuse for not listening. You haven't come this far only to falter in a skill so important to women, have you?

Remember that women are trained to be nicer and more accommodating than men. Don't think that just because she may be less direct in expressing her dissatisfaction or concern over some aspect of the deal that you can ignore it or argue her out of it. Now's the time to put on your listening ears—and eyes. What is really bothering her? Where is her reluctance coming from? By really paying attention to her, you will find out— and can then set about resolving the situation to your mutual satisfaction.

4. Surpass her every expectation.

Simply not pressuring her to close may do more to surpass her expectations than anything else you could do. This is also the ideal time to pull something truly creative and helpful out of your hat—taking action to go that famous "extra mile" that will not only make her life easier but give her something to talk about with friends for years to come.

How do you surpass her expectations? We asked several women and here are their stories.

One luxury car dealership in Michigan hands a woman customer a rose along with the keys to her new car. Now, we can hear you saying "But that's a luxury dealer, we can't compete with them." Sure you can. In these days of warehouse stores offering two dozen roses for less than $20, every dealership should be able to spring for a flower for every women who comes into the dealership. And it doesn't have to be flowers. How about two Godiva chocolates in a tiny, gold box?

You don't have to wait until she's ready to drive off to surpass her expectations. Between the time you close the sale and hand her the keys, you typically have to pass her on to the finance department. While your customer has built trust with you, she's back at Ground Zero with the finance people. That's where you step in. Tell her about what to expect, including all hidden costs above what she's expecting. Reassure her that if she has any questions, you'll be there to answer them for her. And introduce her personally to the finance expert, making sure you share some interesting bit of information you've learned that will make a quick and easy connection. For example, "Mary Ann's an excellent surfer. She just returned from a surfing trip to Hawaii."

A colleague of ours leases her cars from a dealer 110 miles from her home. The salesperson delivers the car, and she signs the papers on her kitchen table. Then, the salesman takes her old lease car and drives it 110 miles back. She's leased three luxury cars from that dealership in the last six years. She lives within five miles of three other dealerships that sell the same brand. You get the idea.

5. Telegraph confidence.

A woman wants a qualified and reliable ally in the sales process, someone who projects both confidence and competence. When you're closing a sale this means being completely on top of your dealership's selling process so that you can confidently lead your customer through it.

Resist the temptation to tug at her heartstrings or guilt-trip her into deciding to buy. Telling her you really need this sale to make your quota is likely not only to make her feel pressured, but to set her wondering how good you are if you feel the need to beg for a sale.

5 STEPS TO A PRESSURE-LESS CLOSE

One of the biggest lessons to learn about closing is the importance of maintaining a balanced attitude.

You need to approach the close in the belief that it is another step in the process of developing a relationship, and not the final step, either. Accept the fact that women are probably going to take longer to make a decision than your male customers. Instead of worrying that you will lose the sale if you don't close now, adopt an attitude of abundance. You will sell your customer eventually—if not today, then tomorrow.

In addition to these "attitude adjustments," there are five specific steps you can take to keep your customer in charge of the selling process so that you can make the sale her way.

1. Drive the process, not her decision.

Although you cannot shorten a woman's buying cycle to meet your needs, you can guide it. Just because you're not pressuring her doesn't mean you should do nothing. While she wants to make the decision on her timetable, she also wants you to ease the process for her. Again, remember that for her this not a transaction; it's a relationship with a trusted adviser.

Let her set the pace by asking what she needs to move forward. Maybe it's more information; maybe it's a review of information you've already provided.

"What additional information can I get for you?"

"What's the best way to get it to you?"

Act as her intermediary with other people or departments so that she gets what she needs. Most of the time this is pretty straightforward—collecting more information, for example, or helping with forms.

If she's trading in a car, walk her out to the used car lot, introduce her to the sales manager, and tell him she'll be in your office when he has a price. If she needs to transfer plates, make the arrangements. One salesperson we know ran over to the license bureau to file the paperwork for a customer because he knew she needed the car the next day and the bureau was going to close at noon. This was a twofer. Not only did he drive the process, he exceeded her expectations.

2. Help her weigh each option.

Plopping down $20-$30,000 for a vehicle is a big deal for most people, so it's no wonder a customer might want to go slow. If she's got a lot to consider, she'll appreciate your help with comparing the various options. One approach that keeps you out of the pushing mode is to go back to the priorities she gave you, and show her how the options measure up.

"I recommended this model because of your concern about driving in snow and bad weather. Is that still a concern?"

"This model has halogen headlights. You mentioned you didn't like your old car because the headlights were so bad that you couldn't see well at night."

Ask her to describe the risks she sees. Don't try to talk her out of them.

"When you think of your investment in this vehicle, what concerns come to mind?"

"You said you didn't want a payment higher than $400 a month. Let's look at the options together and see what we can come up with."

"What would make you feel more secure?"

Walk through the potential gains, downsides, and tradeoffs of each option. Then compare the options with regard to their pluses and minuses.

Offer your best advice only when she asks for it. You may have to bite your tongue to keep from telling her what you think she should do. Try to remember that in helping her come to her own conclusion, you're also continuing to build a relationship that could result in substantial future sales.

Demonstrate optimism, enthusiasm, and patience. Reaffirm that she's making an important decision and is right to be taking her time. Assure her that the approach she's taking will produce a decision she'll be happy with. Offer her your continuing support.

3. Give her some room.

Many women will want some mental breathing space to think, talk with family and friends, and let everything sink in. Give her as much space as she needs. You might want to direct her to a quiet spot where she can review what she's learned.

At the same time, make yourself available, and be sure she has several options for getting in touch with you.

The biggest challenge in waiting for her final decision may be managing your own anxiety. Having invested a lot of your time and energy, it's hard not knowing when or if the deal will go through. One way to reduce your uncertainty is to have already planned what your next move with her will be. Will you follow up with some more information? Give her the name of someone she could talk to?

One dealership we heard about has a computer on the sales floor. It's hooked up to the Internet. They have a list of all the Web sites for their competitor's products. They encourage customers to use the Web to research all the cars that might meet their needs. Sounds a little crazy, but think about it. What better action could you take to build trust? And the customer never leaves the dealership or encounters some fast-talking salesperson who might steal her away.

Suggest a concrete plan for following up. The challenge here is to structure times to talk without crowding her.

"Let's set a time to talk in a day or two to see where things stand. How does that sound?"

"What's the best way to follow up with you?"

Support her desire to involve others in her decision making. Don't take it personally; it doesn't mean that she doesn't trust you or respect your opinion.

4. Help her finalize her decision.

A woman will notice if you start to shift your focus from her to closing the sale. Make sure you stress the importance of the relationship to you by reviewing with her what you've done to arrive at this point. Offer plenty of affirmations that she has made the right decision. Make it clear that you have enjoyed working with her and look forward to working together in the future.

Recap the outcomes she's looking for, and how her decision will provide them.

Nail down any loose ends. She'll appreciate your attention to detail. Incidentally, make sure you find a graceful way to let her know what you've done for her. First, your efforts on her behalf will further cement your relationship. She should know about them, if you can let her know without appearing to brag.

Express your endorsement of her decision. Many buyers have moments of insecurity and doubt after making a major purchase. This is especially true for women in traditionally male industries. Besides, at some level the better she feels about her decision, the better she will feel about you as the person who helped her reach it.

5. Don't allow a "no" to end the process.

If she decides not to move ahead, keep the relationship open. Act as if it will continue. Don't automatically assume that you did something wrong, or that she is not interested in what you are selling. Women lead complicated lives, and there may well be outside factors that are causing her to say no at this particular time.

A luxury car sales associate we heard about ruined a sale by getting suspicious when a woman he had been working with appeared to be backing out of a sale. She was getting a healthy bonus from her company, and was planning to use it to buy herself a car. They'd worked out a price and the features she wanted. She told him she would sign the papers on Friday, when she expected her bonus check to come through.

Her check didn't arrive on Friday, so she called the sales associate to say she'd have to wait until it did. Thinking this was a bargaining ploy on her part, he started applying pressure to buy now, giving her $500 off the price and throwing in leather seats. "It made me angry that he didn't take my word," she said. "I thought we had a pretty good relationship and suddenly he's hustling me. I ended up going elsewhere."

So keep the door open, even if she ends up not buying. She may be feeling guilty for taking so much of your time. Alleviate her concerns by sharing your enthusiasm for working with her in the future.

"I'm sorry this didn't work out, but I enjoyed working with you and hope we can work together in the future."

Create excuses to reach out. This is where your female-focused listening can pay off. If you share a common interest, use it to stay in touch. If she said she liked a certain author, and you read a review of his latest book, send it to her with a brief note.

Some salespeople make a point of having an additional piece of nonessential information they can use as a reason for a follow-up call.

Assume that you will work together in the future, and act accordingly. For example, be sure to include her in occasional mailings you send out.

Finally, ask for her feedback on how you might have met her needs better.

"I'd really appreciate your feedback on what I might have done differently."

Take in what she says, and use it with your other women customers. A customer's honest feedback is a real gift. She's under no obligation to take the time to tell you what she thinks of your performance, so listen with an open mind to everything she says. Don't get defensive, or try to convince her of what you were trying to do. Just take it all in, and when she's done, thank her for her insights.

Pitfalls

Closing is a high-stakes moment; any one of several pitfalls can be enough to spoil the deal.

- ➤ *Assuming she's not the decision-maker.* There's no quicker way to ruin a sale than by hinting that she might not be the decision-maker. So assume she is, until and unless she tells you otherwise.
- ➤ *Misreading her nods.* In earlier chapters we talked about the fact that men nod to express agreement, women to express understanding. As you approach the close, however, you might revert to your default understanding. So be careful: just because you want her to agree, don't assume that she does.
- ➤ *Rushing her.* Anything you do to hurry her along takes away her control of the situation. It also undercuts the impression that you're focused more on the relationship than on the outcome.
- ➤ *Poor-mouthing.* Don't attempt to win her sympathy by hinting at how much you need this sale. It's a manipulation. She won't like it, or respect you for using it.

In conclusion, if you can maintain a positive attitude, focus on what the customer wants and concentrate on nurturing the relationship, you can complete a pressure-less close. One of the outcomes will be a mutual understanding that, in terms of the relationship, it isn't a close at all, but just another step in the buying and selling process.

9 SUPPORTING HER THROUGH THE SALE

How to Provide Seamless, Non-Intrusive Administration

Now that she has decided to buy, is she history? Is your mind racing ahead to the next sale? Are you looking for the earliest possible moment when you can hand her over to the Finance and Insurance department and forget about her?

We hope not.

We know there are dealer principals and sales managers who encourage their sales professionals to pass a customer along as soon as possible, get back out on the floor, and sell, sell, sell. Chances are these folks have never heard of the D-gene.

Once you understand the perspective of a woman customer who has reached this point in her buying process, you'll understand why it's so critical to provide her with continuing support.

For your customer, her decision to buy represents the beginning of a longer-term relationship with you, not the end. At some level she sees everything that has led up to this point almost as a kind of courtship. Her decision to buy is a reward not only for the quality of your recommendations, but also for your attentive listening, and your willingness to *do it her way*. She likes your enthusiasm, and your understanding of the uniqueness of her situation. In short, she has cast her lot with you because you seem to be someone she can trust and work with successfully over the long haul.

> **"I DO"**
>
> *When a woman makes the decision to buy, in her mind it's a little like moving from dating to marriage.*

Women customers and salespeople see the period of time between the decision to buy and the final execution of the sale very differently. Salespeople, having just closed the sale on a car or truck, tend to withdraw their attention and energy from the relationship. From here on in, they would like to think, it's all paperwork. "I've done my job," they think. "The finance people can take care of the rest." Customers, however, are often surprised and sometimes confused by all the decisions as to terms and types of financing that must be made before they actually take possession of the car. Should they buy an extended warranty? What are destination charges? How did a $1,000 down payment turn into $1,750? What do all those lease terms really mean? Would it be smarter to finance through a bank or credit union? Why is the print so small and the ink so light?

> **BECAUSE SHE CAN STILL CHANGE HER MIND**
>
> *After she decides to buy, there are more decisions to make. During this time she needs to know she can continue to rely on you. If you take your eye off the ball, you could lose yourself a customer.*

Remember, a woman sees an automobile dealership as a man's world, and her safety net in that world is the salesperson she's just learned to trust—the one with whom she has a relationship. She doesn't know the folks on the F&I team. They're perfect strangers, and she doesn't trust them any more than she trusted you when she first walked in the door.

So, *friend,* you're still it as far as she's concerned. Nice try if you think you can pass her off and walk away. You can't. Well, let us rephrase that. You *can* walk away from her after the sale. But she'll see it as breaking trust, and the vehicle she bought will be the last one she'll buy from you. And remember how we talked about her network? Well, she'll tell all those folks why she won't buy from you again, too. Now, don't think she's being petty by telling everyone—including the lady getting her hair cut in the next chair at the beauty parlor—how you let her down. She's not. She's just trying to keep them from working with someone who's less than trustworthy.

You are smarter than that. You've made it to Chapter 9. So, let's look at how you pass her off with out ticking her off.

EXTENDING THE RELATIONSHIP TO THE F&I TEAM: WHAT THE SALESPERSON CAN DO

Even though her primary relationship is with you, in order to execute the sale she may need to work with others in your organization to complete the sale. Special treatment is exactly what women want. And this is where your creativity comes into play. During this part of the selling process, your understanding of the D-gene presents you with an unequaled opportunity to provide the kind of service that will set you apart from your competition. This is your chance to build her confidence that she made the right decision. Here is where you begin to add real value in the form of the peace of mind you create for her—starting with the way you introduce her to your dealership's F&I team.

Here are some steps you can take to extend the relationship to that department:

➤ Explain what the Finance & Insurance Department does, and how it will help her with the particular details of her sale or lease. Briefly mention the kinds of products she may be offered.

➤ Introduce her to the F&I manager, or to the specific person in F&I she will be working with. As you did with the service department, mention some of the details about her that will help F&I understand her overall needs.

"John, I'm leaving Helen, my very favorite investment banker, in your hands."

"John, Harriet is the mother of twins, and I assured her that as the father of twins, you'd be the best guy to help her."

➤ Mention to the F&I person any questions or concerns the customer raised with you. Before you leave, make sure he or she understands the customer's overall needs that are behind these concerns, and is able to answer them to the customer's satisfaction. That may sound something like this:

"Mike, Liz had a really bad experience with the finance people the last time she leased a car. She said she felt like they were putting something over on her, her and she couldn't figure out what it was. I assured her we don't do that kind of thing here."

➤ Make sure the customer knows she can continue to come to you if she needs to. Let her know you hope your relationship her will continue. Say something like:

"Mary, as soon as you've signed all the papers, I'll come get you and we'll go back and meet the people in the service department. Even if it's three years from now, I'm your contact here at Gracious Motors."

EXTENDING THE RELATIONSHIP TO THE F&I TEAM: WHAT THE F&I PERSON CAN DO

Your job is not just to see that the paperwork is filled out and the extended warranties are sold. Your job is to make sure that your secure, happy women customer stays that way. You and the salesperson need to work together closely to expand the customer's relationship to include F&I. You're going to tap into the relationship she has with her salesperson and make it rub off on you. Here are a few things you can do to make the transition as smooth as possible:

➤ Help the salesperson make the introductions as smooth and graceful as possible. Think of what you're doing as meeting the good friend of another good friend. Say something that shows you and the salesperson have talked:

"Mary, Joe told me he'd chosen me to work with his favorite soccer Mom. I've been looking forward to meeting you."

➤ Before the salesman leaves, make sure you understand something of the customer's overall situation, as well as any specific concerns or questions she may have. Assure the salesperson that, as a friend of a friend, his or her customer will be in good hands.

"Joe, I know how you like to make sure your special customers are well taken care of. Helen's in good hands. I'll bring her back to your desk when we're through."

➤ Take time to make sure the customer understands all the steps involved in drawing up the contract, and arranging terms.

"Beth, I know that many of the contracts I'm going to have you sign are unfamiliar. I'll explain what each means. Stop me any time and ask me any questions before you sign. I want you to be absolutely comfortable with what you're signing and why."

"Mrs. Adler, Joe told me that your husband died recently and this is the first car you've ever bought on your own. I am so sorry. It must be a difficult time in your life. I'll try to make this as easy as I can."

➤ Check to make sure there are no major surprises for her in what you are saying. This is the point at which many customers are most suspicious of being taken advantage of. Any deviation from her understanding could send her out the door.

"Jane, I'm going to go through all the paperwork with you. I don't want you to sign anything until you understand what you're signing. So, stop me with any questions."

➤ If misunderstandings do arise, consider conducting a three-way conversation with the car salesperson—with whom her relationship may be stronger.

"Rebecca, I'm not sure what happened with the monthly lease payment. I'm so glad you pointed that out. Let's get Joe over here, and see if he can help us through this."

➤ Ask yourself if there's anything you could do to make your part of the car-buying process easier for her. Can you bring the paperwork to her office or home? Can you deliver the car?

"I know that you are going to finance this through your credit union. Here's my card with my direct number. Have the loan officer call me, and I'll give him all the figures that we've just gone over. No, reason for you to have to hassle with all the numbers or run back and forth."

NO TIME TO RELAX

Given everything you've done for her so far, you can be sure she will expect a high level of commitment from everyone else in the dealership. She's going to be very alert to any indication that the primary focus was the sale, and not the relationship. You need to be as energetic and committed as you were before. Your efforts will build trust and loyalty in the short term and positive word of mouth in the long term.

BE HER AMBASSADOR

Does this situation sound familiar?

Mary has finished her meeting with John in F&I. She's ready to pick up her car. Unfortunately, it's still back in the prep area, and the folks back there tell you it's going to be another hour.

You know Mary is busy and has to get home to her family. Although she hasn't said anything, you know that she is the poster child of soccer moms and has a set of twins at home. She spends a lot of time carpooling. She might even have planned on picking up the kids in her new car. You know she's not going to be a happy camper if she has to sit at your desk or in the customer lounge and wait. But more important, you know that letting her wait could well damage the relationship you've worked so hard to build with her. So, what do you do?

Then, it comes to you. After Mary gets the car, you have to show her how to do things like set the radio stations, work the navigation system, pop the trunk, and all the other things the owner of a new car has to learn in order to become comfortable with a new vehicle.

Fortunately for you, there's a demo car with almost all of the same features sitting out in front of the showroom. You act fast. You grab the keys from the board and approach Mary. Remembering everything you've learned about building trust, you say: "Mary, we've run into a small glitch. Your car's still being prepped. I know how valuable your time is, so I've got the keys to our demo that's parked right out in front, and I'll walk you through all the features on the demo. That way when you car comes out, you can just get in and go. And John over in F&I said he'd keep on the prep folks while I'm working with you. Will that work for you?"

You brilliant guy, you! Look at how many principles of selling to woman you put to work in one short conversation: You've respected her time. You've told her the truth. You've used the info you learned about her to relate what you were doing to her particular situation, and you've pulled John, whom she now knows, into the relationship. And—drum roll please—you haven't abandoned her after the sale.

If you could read her mind, you'd know that you have done it right. She remains a happy customer, more convinced than ever that she's working with the right person.

And if after you've shown her how to work all the whistles and bells on the demo, her car still isn't ready, there's always a trip over to the service area to introduce her to the manager, the write-up person, and anyone else you think she should know. It's also a good time to explain how to make an appointment, the policy on loaners, and any scheduled maintenance issues she should know.

DELIVER COMFORT, NOT STRESS

Because women are hard-wired for nurturing, many spend their lives caring for other people. They have husbands, kids, partners, parents, and friends who depend on them. So imagine the appreciation they'll feel when they know you are looking out for their best interests. Anything you can do to lighten the load will make a big difference to a woman, both in terms of time and effort saved, and the psychological security that comes from knowing you are her champion.

Return with us now to the service area. The service manager is telling Mary about oil changes, tire rotations, and other scheduled maintenance issues. Because you're still tuned in with your listening ears and eyes, you see Mary's eyes beginning to glaze over. She tuned out somewhere between having the hoses checked at 24,000 miles and the need for rotating the tires every 3,000 miles. So, as you and Mary head back to your desk, you say:

> *"Boy, there's a lot to remember, isn't there? Most of it is in the owner's manual, but if you've got any questions, just give me a call. I've been doing this a long time."*

Some salespeople tend to stress the problems and difficulties involved, in order to make their efforts to help seem more impressive. It's certainly acceptable to let her know what you're doing on her behalf, but ratcheting up her anxiety level is not a good idea.

Here is a brief list of phrases that create anxiety, along with examples of what you can say instead.

WORDS THAT CREATE ANXIETY	WORDS THAT MAKE HER FEEL COMFORTABLE
I'm afraid that isn't going to work.	Let me see what I can do to make that work for you.
That's not our policy.	I'll talk to a few people, and see what we can work out. We want you to be happy.
You'll have to check with your lender.	I'd be happy to get that information for you.
There's usually a long wait.	I'll personally walk your application through our office.
We've never done that before.	Let's see if it's do-able.
You need to submit that by the 15th or it won't go through.	We can draw up the paperwork for you. Then you can approve it and we'll submit it.

If something goes wrong, make sure it's taken care of promptly. Apologize to her right away, even if it wasn't your fault. Taking personal responsibility will reinforce in her mind that you value your relationship with her and are doing whatever it takes to make her experience with you and the dealership one of mutual respect.

Pitfalls

➤ *Over-explaining.* Assume that she's a busy person, and limit explanations accordingly. Executing the sale may involve many steps, but unless she makes a specific request for information, she doesn't need to know all the details.

➤ *Losing your focus.* Stay involved. If you're just going through the motions, she'll pick it up. After-sale support is not something you can provide with half your brain engaged—not the kind of thoughtful and proactive help that will delight her and have her singing your praises to her friends and colleagues.

STAYING IN TOUCH

How to Build an Enhanced Relationship with Her and Hers

If you've been applying the concepts of this book to your women customers, by now you should be sitting on a gold mine of potential new business.

As anyone in sales or marketing can tell you, *the best customer is a returning customer*—for all the obvious reasons. After all, you already have a relationship, she trusts you, and you know what she needs. There is also the cost angle. Depending on the industry, it can cost anywhere from two to forty times more to acquire a new customer than to keep an old one.[1]

The next best customer is someone referred to you by an existing customer. Compared to walk-in customers or those developed through cold calling or direct marketing, referrals are always more cost-effective. They require less convincing, they make the decision to buy faster, they tend to generate repeat business, and they are themselves more likely to refer you to others.[2] And that applies to customers of both genders.

> *A satisfied woman customer is a veritable referral machine.*

A satisfied woman customer is a veritable referral machine. In general, a woman will share her experiences more than a man, and in more detail. She values relationships and likes to be helpful.

---

[1] Rhonda Abrams, *New Business from Old Clients,* Inc.com April 2002

[2] Richard Banfield, *How Referral Marketing Can Grow Your Profits,* On Track Coaching & Consulting Inc. 2003

It's a winning combination. If you have helped your woman customer, she will need little encouragement from you to let her friends and families know what you did for her, and how you can help them. And if you've surpassed her expectations, she'll rave to her friends about you. She will want to help you build a strong customer base.

There's a term for what a woman does when she shares information about you with her network of friends. It's called *word-of-mouth marketing,* and it's the most important and compelling form of marketing communication. People perceive word-of-mouth messages to be credible, trustworthy, and without hidden motives. What's more, the recipients of word-of-mouth messages typically pass them on to other people they know.[3]

Do the math. If 25 people tell 25 people and the process is repeated five more times, the number is comes close to equaling the population of the United States. You won't get that many referrals, but how about a dozen, or fifty, or a hundred? A satisfied woman customer is one of the most powerful—and least appreciated—generators of extraordinary sales results. Think of the complex lives women lead. Each of your women customers is a potential point of entry to several markets including family members, friends, colleagues, community organizations, and businesses. In short, whatever you can do to sustain and enrich your relationship with her will be effort well spent, both in terms of the business she will give you and the connections she will create for you with people in her networks.

In addition to nurturing the relationship, one of the reasons we talk so much about going the extra mile for your women customers is that special treatment gives them something to talk about with other people. A woman we know went to a department store to buy her husband a blue shirt with a white collar.

[3] Michael Cafferky, *Let Your Customers Do the Talking.* Dearborn Trade, 1995

She'd seen one in their catalog and she knew he would like it, but the store was out of his size.

Noticing her disappointment, the saleswoman said, "If you can wait until tomorrow, I'll have something for you."

The next day, when the wife went back to the store, the saleswoman presented her with a blue shirt with a white collar in her husband's size. "That's fantastic!" said the wife. "Where'd you get it?"

"Actually, I made it," the saleswoman said. "I took home a blue shirt and a white shirt in the same style in his size. I replaced the blue collar on the blue shirt with the white collar from the white shirt. Voila! A blue shirt with a white collar."

That was years ago, and the woman is still dining out on this stellar example of a sales professional going the extra mile. Wouldn't you love to be in that category with your women clients? Can't you hear them saying, "You think that was great service? Let me tell you about Bob over at XYZ Auto Sales. When I bought my last new car, he … " (you finish it).

Here are some suggestions aimed at maintaining great relationships with your customers.

STAY IN TOUCH WITH HER—EVEN WHEN YOU DON'T WANT ANYTHING

Knowing how, and how often, to contact a woman customer is a delicate matter. On the one hand, women are busy. They can't afford to waste time in purposeless activity, and they will resent any implication on your part that they are just sitting around. On the other hand, women like to know you're thinking about them, especially when you don't have anything to sell them.

If you've been paying attention, you have discovered points of intersection between her life and interests and yours. Perhaps

BE REALISTIC ABOUT WHAT YOU CAN DO

When you're just starting out, you'll probably have plenty of time to stay in touch. As you get more customers, you may have less time. This is when small-group events can work for you—as long as they feel personal.

you attend the same church or your kids go to the same school. Maybe you grew up in the same town or cheer for the same sports team. Any interest you share presents an opportunity for maintaining and enhancing the relationship you so carefully built. Sending her a book on a subject of common interest, for example, or letting her know about an upcoming event that you think she'd like makes her feel special.

For the savvy salesperson, the customer's ongoing service experience with the dealership offers the best avenue for maintaining personal contact. Many dealerships have software that enables salespeople to track all kinds of customer information—birthdays, anniversaries of purchases, due dates for leases, and when the customer will be bringing the car in for service.

Says the sales manager at a luxury car dealership, "A good salesperson will find out when a customer is coming in for service. He'll walk back when she comes in to say hello and make sure there are no problems. He may visit again during the day to see that the service is proceeding on schedule. And he'll be there, if only briefly, when she picks the car up. If she's had the car for two or three years, he may mention something about the new models that he thinks would meet her particular needs, but his main purpose is to keep their relationship going."

Here are some other ways the top salespeople keep in touch with their female customers:

> *Check on prospects who ended up buying or leasing cars from a competitor.* "I make a point of calling people who came in here but ended up buying or leasing a car from a competitor," said a saleswoman. "I want to know what they thought of the car they bought or leased, what problems they had, that sort of thing. They appreciate the fact that

I remembered them enough to call, and I'm often able to construct a deal for their next car that works better for them than what they had."

➤ *Make referrals to a competitor to keep a customer happy.* One salesman had a long-time customer who said she had driven Audis for 15 years and wanted to try something different. Was there anyone at the local BMW dealership he could recommend talking to? "I probably could have talked her out of it," the salesman remembers, "but I figured we'd known each other for 15 years and I was sure I'd be selling her cars again in the future. Besides, I kind of knew what she meant. She wanted a change."

➤ *Give her tickets to local events.* One successful salesperson sends the customers free tickets to local events he knows they'll like. He buys season tickets to a community theater group and gives them to customers who like live theater. They're not Broadway tickets, but they work just as well. He does the same with tickets to the auto show. "I don't just send them coupons for a few dollars off," he said. " I pay the extra $5 or $6, so it costs them nothing but the parking. He and his wife had tickets to a fundraiser for the local Humane Society. They couldn't attend, so he gave the ticket to a customer who loves dogs as much as they do. But he doesn't just drop the tickets in an envelope. He calls first to see if his customer can use the tickets.

➤ *Call to see how things are going.* "I always call a customer within the first week," said a salesperson. " I ask how she likes her new vehicle and if she has any questions about any of the features. Almost always, they're having problems with something that I can help them with. Last week, a woman was having trouble with her On Star system. I knew the On Star advisors could have helped her, but she came in, and I helped her. What can I say, she loves me!" the salesperson said with a laugh.

Your dealership may have someone who makes these phone calls, but that's not good enough. Your customer has a relationship with you, not someone being paid to read a script. If you know she brought the car or truck in for service, call to see if everything went well. Again, the dealership does this, but she'll appreciate hearing from you too.

Women like to bond with each other. They like to think of themselves as part of your family of customers. You can strengthen this perception, along with your role of trusted adviser or financial planner, by hosting small social events (no selling involved). In addition to sharing something of yourself to strengthen your customer relationships, you're also putting yourself in the position where you can keep up with events in your customers' lives that may affect their plans for buying their next vehicle.

One car salesperson we know had a daughter the same age as a customer's son. The son was enrolled in a specialized program at a large university. The salesperson's daughter was interested in applying to the same program, but she didn't know anyone in it. The salesperson invited the customer and her son out to lunch with him and his daughter. The daughter got into the program, and the salesperson made a life-long friend and loyal customer.

More and more dealerships are offering "customer appreciation" events, often focused on the introduction of new models. Many of these are for men and women, and are designed to appeal to both genders.

One dealership made a deal with a local music store to raffle off a black baby grand piano at a special event. Until then the piano sat in the showroom. Every once in a while a customer would sit down and try it out. On Saturday afternoon the dealership hired a professional pianist. Said one woman customer, "It was very pleasant, having the piano music in the background. It elevated the whole experience, somehow."

Another dealer had a party for their women customers, with appropriate prizes, to showcase female-friendly car models. Some dealerships add activities like massages or fashion shows.

If your dealership is planning such an event, call or send personal notes to your women customers saying you hope they'll attend. Let them know it's okay to bring a friend. And make it clear that you won't be doing any hard selling at gatherings like these. You just want to stay in touch and get to know them better.

> *"Hi, Rachel, this is Bob at XYZ. I just wanted to let you know that we're having an event for our women customers here next Sunday afternoon. A massage therapist is going to be giving free head and neck massages and there will be five or six manicurists and make-up artists giving free makeovers. Now, I won't kid you, it's meant to bring women into showroom, so we can sell them cars. But you already bought a car from us, and I thought you should have the opportunity to get some free pampering too."*

Let's stop for a moment and look at what Bob just said—without having to say it. His phone call told Rachel that he remembered her and valued her enough to offer her an opportunity for some pampering, not because he wanted to sell her anything, but because she had bought something and he appreciated it.

Staying in touch doesn't have to be elaborate. More modest suggestions include the following:

➤ Visit, phone, or send an e-mail one week after a sale to make sure she's delighted with her new vehicle—and to take care of any problems that may have come up.

➤ Send a note thanking her for her business. Use your own stationery.

➤ Return her calls within three hours, and always on the same day.

➤ Send a newsletter with items of interest to women. Be sure to add a hand-written note or something else to personalize it.

➤ Send holiday and birthday cards. Personalize them in some way. Hint: don't send cards your dealer buys in bulk—they're the opposite of personal.

The key to staying in touch, whatever form it takes, is to make it *personal.* It's adding a *personal* note to a newsletter, making a *personal* call, sending a card with a *personal* note. The better you've been at female-friendly listening, the more you'll be able to find just the right message to let her know you understand her situation and value her friendship.

KEEP HER ON YOUR CALENDAR

Knowing that, on average, people in the U. S. buy a car every 42 months should tell you when to make sure to get in touch with your customers.

➤ Call a few months before their lease is up to ask about their experience and discuss plans for their next vehicle.

➤ Create "tickler dates" on your calendar based on what you've learned about their plans and their families. Is a child going off to college this September? Is she in the market for a used car? Might her mother be interested in buying a new car and giving her daughter her old one? You'll never know if you don't give her a call in July or August.

ENCOURAGE HER TO SUPPORT YOUR EFFORTS

Women love to support people who have provided excellent service to them. It's the nurturing part of the D-gene coming out. In other words, you don't need to push women to send you referrals; such hard-ball tactics could even backfire. On the other hand, because she's so busy, you might need to help her focus her efforts on your behalf. Emphasize your enthusiasm for your work, and your interest in helping others:

"One of the things I enjoy about this job is being able to help people like you get the vehicles that are right for them."

"If you know other people I might be able to help, I hope you'll let me know."

Find ways to work statements like this into casual conversation. Suppose you've just delivered a car to Sara. She is so excited about her new car. As you're saying goodbye, she says, " I don't know how to thank you. For the first time in my life, I enjoyed working with a car salesman!" She's just given you the perfect opening to casually tell her you'd like to tap into her network. You say something like:

"Thank you. I enjoyed working with you too. One of the things I like about this job is being able to help people like you get the vehicles that are right for them. If you know other people I might be able to help, I hope you'll let me know or send them my way."

We know that statements like that sound so simple. And they are. You've probably said something like that somewhere along the line. But our experience is that most salespeople say it with no finesse at all. Sara gave you the perfect opening. Had you said this to her as a by-the-way as she was driving out of the dealership, she might have seen it as pushy. Look for the openings.

TRAVEL IN THE CIRCLES SHE DOES

For obvious reasons, the most effective sales professionals are usually those who lead an active and varied life, have several interests they pursue, and come in contact with people from many different walks of life. Not only do these activities help them maintain a balanced outlook on their life, it also expands the pool of possible new customers, and raises the likelihood of their crossing paths with existing customers.

And if your goal is to meet potential women customers, it's smart to go where the women are. Here are some things you can do to express your interests, in ways that will appeal to women:

> *Volunteer.* Women do a lot of volunteer work, and are impressed by men who do the same. What types of organizations or issues would you like to get involved in? Animal rights? Domestic abuse issues? Historical preservation? Nature conservation? Don't forget your child's school or your place of worship.
>
> Years ago, when one of our colleagues was president of the local PTA, she talked a local dealership into letting the group use the showroom for an art auction. Over 200 people were there. And not one salesperson attended. Neither did the dealer.
>
> "I wondered," she said, "why one or two didn't show up. They didn't have to sell anything, they could have shown up and worked the room as unofficial hosts and helped us out with finding things like the floor outlet where we could plug in the coffee pot. We would have liked to get to know them. Instead, the showroom greeter was there, but no one else."

➤ *Learn about women's issues.* Read some books. Check out some newsletters. Listen to what the thought leaders have to say. You'll get a better sense of your present and potential women customers, and you may be able to do some good at the same time.

➤ *Be a resource in your community.* The first thing a woman does when she's looking for something is to call a person who knows what's going on—someone who's well connected. Be that knowledgeable person. Be the one who knows the time the high school football games start and the dates of the annual art fair. Be the one she calls for a reference for a good plumber. And be the one she calls when she's thinking of buying a new car or truck.

➤ *Work in your community.* Find local organizations that need your help, and join them. Make it your business to stay abreast of what's happening in your area: events, theatrical programs, exhibits, educational offerings, trips. You'll soon become known as the go-to guy for customers looking for a special class, a summer program for their 'tween-age child, or what to do with visiting relatives.

➤ *Stand for something.* If, in the course of your volunteer and community work, you discover a cause or an organization you feel strongly about, develop this interest. Follow your passion, as the saying goes. In time you will become identified with this interest, and people will be drawn to you because of it. Do it because you really care and not because it will sell cars and trucks. Women respect people who are making a difference. And you know what? Selling more cars and trucks will follow.

SELLING TO COUPLES

How to Connect with Both Parties

Does decoding the D-gene help you sell to couples?

Absolutely. Understanding the D-gene will increase your awareness of what the woman might be thinking and feeling, and how you can best meet her needs and make her feel comfortable.

However, many times you're not only working with women. Often there's a spouse or partner involved in the process. Together, a couple presents some special challenges. Some of these simply have to do with the fact that you may be having a conversation with a man and a woman at the same time. Others are created by the dynamics between partners—some predictable, others unique to each couple.

> **OUTSIDERS BEWARE!**
> *For many if not most couples, money is a vehicle for relating. A discussion of money, therefore, may not be only a discussion about money. It may be an arena for expressing the emotional dynamics of the relationship.*

Selling to a couple may be the biggest single selling challenge a sales professional faces. Small wonder. When you sell to a couple, you're dealing with two genders that:

➤ Communicate differently
➤ Relate to other people differently
➤ Take in and process information differently
➤ Make decisions differently

Added to that blend, you need to factor in the anxiety that surrounds the whole car-buying experience and, possibly, matrimonial baggage you have no idea about. It's a potentially combustible mixture.

APPEARANCES ARE USUALLY DECEIVING

Gone are the days when the husband made all the decisions and the "little woman" concurred. More and more major purchases involve both spouses. And next to their home, a vehicle is probably one of the largest purchases a couple makes. In fact most car salespeople today realize that women are powerful partners in the buying process, and have a veto power that a salesperson ignores at his peril.

However, awareness of a general trend and the ability to deal with it effectively in a selling situation are two different things. In this context things are seldom what they seem, and often it's awkward to ask any clarifying questions.

Neil, a young auto sales professional in one of our seminars, told a story on himself that illustrates this point.

A couple in their late 30's had come in looking for a four-door sedan. As a real estate agent, the wife was going be the primary driver of the vehicle, although it would also be used as the family car. Neil got the impression that she was going to buy the car in her name, so he tried to direct most of his initial questions to her. This proved to be somewhat difficult, because her husband had done a lot of preliminary research, some of it on the Internet, and seemed to have strong ideas about what his wife needed.

He showed them several models, and they both test-drove two or three. It became apparent that the husband was very concerned about the environment, and the future price of gas, and was pushing the wife towards the smaller, lower-end models. She agreed with his concern, but Neil noticed her eyes lighting up when they stopped briefly to look at an SUV with a luxury package.

Wanting to be responsive to the woman, who he thought would be the primary driver, he asked her what she liked about it. "Well," she said, "it looks like it would be a more comfortable care for my clients to get in and out of easily, and they'd ride more comfortably too."

The husband frowned. "I'm just concerned that if gas continues to go up, people will be embarrassed to be seen in a car like that," he said.

The wife nodded, and agreed that a smaller sedan probably made more sense.

At some point after that, the husband went out to their car to get some papers, and the wife started talking to Neil about the SUV she had liked. He agreed with her that it would be good for driving clients around. As they talked, he thought to himself that since she was buying the car with her money, it seemed to him only fair that she should get something that met her needs. When her husband returned, she said she wanted to test-drive the SUV.

"Also," Neil chimed in, "it comes with a navigation system, which would really help you get around town without having to get out a map or ask directions."

"You can buy those things at any electronics store and just attach them to the windshield," the husband replied, "and they're much cheaper."

Neil saw the look of disappointment that crossed the wife's face. He caught her eye and shrugged sympathetically.

That was the essentially end of the conversation. They left quickly, saying they would think everything over. In the next day or two Neil called them a few times, but was not surprised when neither husband nor wife returned his calls. He realized that the sale was not going to happen.

WHAT WENT WRONG?

Neil had thought that since it was going to be the wife's car, bought with her money, she deserved to get what she liked. He saw himself as giving her a voice, validating her comments and helping her stand up to her husband. What he hadn't bargained for was that the wife was protective of her husband, and felt more strongly about not "ganging up" on him than she did about getting the vehicle she wanted. Neil had tuned into what the wife wanted in the way of a car, but he hadn't picked up on her need to make sure she didn't humiliate her husband by siding against him.

Many women will defer to their husbands in public. They may have strong opinions, they may have more technical knowledge, they may be movers and shakers in their professional lives, but in public they may feel more comfortable letting their husbands take the lead. Do they not want to appear unfeminine? Do they fear damaging their husbands' fragile male egos? Who knows? For our purposes, it doesn't really matter.

What about the husband? Was he really so concerned about renewable resources? Or did he resent that she was the primary breadwinner in the family? Maybe to make their life easier, she did everything she could to make him feel that he was in charge. Maybe. We'll never know. All we know is that Neil somehow got himself aligned with the wife, which made it appear that he was aligned against the husband.

So, what should Neil have done? Well, for starters he should not have made any assumptions. He assumed that the wife was going to be the decision maker because it was going to be her car. He was wrong. On the other hand, how many times have you had a husband and wife come in and assumed he was going to be the decision maker, only to find out that while he wanted a truck with an extended cab, she wanted a minivan, and they got the van. Today, women influence over 85 percent of all buying decisions.

Have you ever heard someone say, "Never get between a mother bear and her cub"? The same rule applies when dealing with spouses. Don't get in the middle of disagreements between husbands and wives. Don't take sides. Let them figure it out, or fight it out in their own way. Let's look at a few things Neil could have done to avoid getting caught in the middle.

Neil could have listened and observed more closely. There were clues all over the place that could have helped him. Who was it who arrived with all the information and had been researching on line? It wasn't the wife. Who held the strongest opinions on the type of car? It wasn't the wife. Who waited until hubby was out earshot before asking questions? That was the wife. If she had all the power, why did she wait until her husband was out of the room to discuss the SUV? Red flag. Red flag. Something's going on here, and Neil didn't know what it was.

We know that Neil didn't do thorough enough groundwork into the couple's needs. So, is there any way he could have gotten himself out of the middle as the drama played out?

For starters, he could have responded to each spouse's comments by reflecting what each said and giving product information without taking sides. Let's look at how this works.

Husband says, " I'm concerned about rising oil prices.

Neil says, "Many people share your concerns. This model right here gets 30 miles to the gallon on the highway, and has received the highest customer satisfaction ratings, and there is one diesel model available if that works for you."

Wife says, "This SUV would be more comfortable and easier to get in and out of than the smaller car."

Neil says, " I've heard people say that it's a very comfortable car, and for an SUV, it is easy to get in and out of."

Husband says, "If gas prices go up, people will be embarrassed to be seen in a car like that."

Neil responds, "Changes in the economy do tend to make some people uncomfortable to be seen in certain vehicles. All I can say is that this SUV gets about 26 miles to the gallon on the highway."

Get it? Neil simply restates what the customer says and adds any information that will help them clarify their thinking and come to their own decision.

COUPLESPEAK / TRANSLATING WOMEN	
Yes.	= No.
No.	= Yes.
Maybe.	= No.
I'm sorry.	= You'll be sorry.
We need...	= I want...
It's your decision.	= The correct decision should be obvious by now.
Do what you want.	= You'll pay for this later.
We need to talk.	= I need to complain.
Sure... go ahead.	= I don't want you to.
I'm not upset.	= You'd better believe I'm upset.
I'll be ready in a minute.	= Kick off your shoes and find a good game on TV.
You have to learn to communicate.	= Just agree with me.
Are you listening to me!?	= Too late, you're dead.
In response to: "What's wrong?" Nothing.	= Everything.

COUPLESPEAK / TRANSLATING MEN	
It's a guy thing.	= There is no rational thought pattern connected with it, and you have no chance at all of making it logical.
Uh huh, sure, Honey. (or its equivalent,) Yes, Dear.	= Absolutely nothing. It's a conditioned response.
It would take too long to explain.	= I have no idea how it works. (or) I have no idea what I'm talking about.
That's interesting, Dear.	= Are you still talking. (or) I hope she didn't notice I was falling asleep while she was talking.
Hey, I've got my reasons for what I'm doing.	= And I sure hope I think of some pretty soon.

GUIDING A COUPLE'S BUYING EXPERIENCE

Your goal for managing a conversation with a husband and wife should be to find a way to communicate with both of them, identify and build on areas of agreement, and avoid getting caught up in the dynamics between them. It's a good idea early in your initial conversation with them to ask each person to state the reason he or she came to see you. You can say something like:

> *"I can be of more help in directing you to one of our vehicles, if I have an idea of what each of you wants in the car you're looking for. Let me take a few notes as we talk. Sharon, how about if I start with you? What do you see as the perfect car?"*

This will give you a good idea of how in sync they are. If they can't agree on a broad generality, chances are the discussion isn't going to get easier once you get into specifics. You don't want to underscore differences, but it will help you to know how they differ in their views on what's important in the car they want to buy.

If they're in agreement now but disagree as the process continues, you can refer to some common goals to help get the discussion back on track. For example, if the spouses have agreed on their maximum monthly payment, you can use this agreement to help them resolve a disagreement on specific features. As your discussions continue, take every opportunity to restate their positions in terms that highlight areas of agreement:

> *"This model has the safety features you both agreed were important."*

If they agree with each other but not with you, feel free to represent your point of view. If they disagree with each other, don't be like Neil. Stand back. Don't try to convince them of either position. Instead, think of yourself as an educator or a facilitator, bringing up relevant information, summarizing their positions as they evolve, and, again, always looking for areas of agreement.

SOME OTHER DO'S AND DON'TS

Dealing with some couples can feel as if you're walking through a minefield, but the fact is, many of your customers are couples (even if you only deal with one half) and you will need to know how to navigate successfully. Fortunately, there are some guidelines you can follow that will help you increase your chances of success—even with the toughest of couples.

> ➤ *Shake hands with both of them.* Don't lose any sleep over the "shaking hands" issue. It doesn't matter whose hand you shake first. Start with the person who is closest to you. Don't make a fool of yourself by going around the husband to shake the wife's hand first—or vice versa.

> ➤ *Until they tell you differently, assume both spouses are equally involved in all phases of the buying process, even if they don't appear to be.* The question is, where does the decision-making power lie? Who has the power to kill the deal? Until you know for sure, it's easier, and safer, to assume they are equal partners. And remember, what they say and what they do may be very different.

> ➤ *Pay equal attention to each spouse.* This isn't always easy, especially if one spouse is much more responsive than the other, but if you can't figure out a way to do it, you'll quickly get yourself in hot water. If you pay more attention to the wife, for example, she'll be sensitive to the poor treatment her husband is getting, and will side with him against you.

➤ *If you pay more attention to the man, on the other hand, she'll assume you're ignoring her because she is a woman.* Ignoring the woman is a deal-breaker, although neither spouse may ever say so.

➤ *Think about visuals.* Use what you know about the D-gene to make sure your visuals appeal to women as well as men. Also, if you use charts or brochures, make sure both spouses can easily see them. Many salespeople have two sets prepared, one for each spouse. If you decide to do this, by all means prepare them ahead of time. If you stop the meeting to get a second set of materials, one of the spouses will think he or she was an afterthought. For your sake, we hope it's not the wife.

➤ *Use inclusive language when you answer their questions.* Even though one spouse may have asked a question, frame your answer in a way that will appeal to the other spouse as well. Use phrases like "you both" or "your family." Make eye contact with both spouses as you speak. Whenever possible, create bridges back to what both spouses said. Keep the focus on both of them.

"Before we go any further, I want to make sure you're both comfortable with the financing we talked about. Jack, you said you couldn't go higher than $350 a month and Jill you thought $400. What we've been discussing comes out to $425, and I can't get it lower unless we spread the payments over 48 months rather than 36. What do you think?"

➤ *Beware of slipping into your male default mode.* Even though you may have mastered female-friendly listening, focusing on the relationship, and all the other D-gene skills, they can seem a little awkward when you're talking to a man as well as a woman. Some male sales professionals feel the need to let the man know they are still one of the guys, and also that they are not hitting on his wife, so they treat her like she's not there. Hitting on the wife is probably not an issue when you're discussing turbo-charged engines, but ignoring the wife is an issue no matter what you're discussing. The real danger is in connecting with him in a way that excludes her.

➤ *Never provide the husband with information or a "goodie" you don't also offer the wife.* Some car dealership service departments automatically offer a man a loaner car, whereas they will give a woman one only if she asks. If a woman has to ask for something that you automatically offer her husband, you are, as the kids would say, toast! They'll both be angry—she for the obvious reasons, he on her behalf. He also knows that every time this dealership comes up in conversation, she's going to tell him how biased it is against women.

➤ *Never turn her down when she requests something, and then reverse yourself when her husband calls.* You don't want to leave the impression that you take him more seriously than you take her. If you won't go to the trouble to get a certain set of figures for her but you will for him, that's exactly the impression you will leave. If you can't find a car in the area to make a dealer trade for her, but you come through for him, be prepared to eat that trade. She'll nix the deal so fast it will make your head spin.

➤ *Don't try to psych out their relationship.* You can't. No one knows what goes on behind closed doors, but you can be sure it's more than meets the eye. Your safest position is simply to treat them both as your customers.

➤ *Never, ever, take sides.* Seen that before in this chapter? Did you ever have a friend who told you he and his wife had separated? And you offered your support by saying,

in effect, that you never liked her very much anyway—
oops!—only to have them get back together? This is the
danger of siding with one spouse over the over.

Taking sides, or appearing to take sides, which has the
same effect, is easier to fall into than you might think.
You're taking sides when:

- You support the husband as he tries to convince his
  wife to accept your recommendation.
- You correct one spouse.
- You nod, smile or in some other nonverbal way let
  the couple know which spouse you agree with.

➤ *Leave them alone.* When a couple disagrees, it's a good
idea for you to retire from the scene and give them time
to talk in private. In this way you can avoid getting
sucked into the middle of an argument. Besides, it may
be easier for them to reach agreement without the pres-
ence of a third party.

GETTING RICH

This book is about how to get RICH selling cars and trucks to women, right? That's what the title implies. So is that all there is to it? Now that you've read the book, you'll be living the lavish lifestyle, buying a bigger home, driving a luxury car, and vacationing with the rich and famous. Why not?

IT TAKES PRACTICE

Actually, there's one more thing that's required. It's important and something you'll need to take seriously. So just to lighten up a little, have you heard the one about the visitor who approached a native New Yorker on Fifth Avenue and asked him, "Tell me, how do you get to Carnegie Hall?" Without breaking stride, the New Yorker responded, "practice, practice, practice". Okay, it's an old joke, but it makes the point. How many world-class musicians, artists, and athletes have been able to improve their performance simply by reading books on the subject?

Right. Zero. In other words, now that you've read about how to sell to women, it's time to go out and start putting what you know to work, testing the skills and concepts in this book, noticing how your customers respond, and making whatever adjustments seem necessary to get the results you're looking for. You won't change completely overnight, and you may feel awkward at first, but as these new behaviors become more comfortable, you will begin to notice positive results.

The key is to find the practice mode that works best for you. For some people, putting the concepts of this book into practice will require nothing more than a series of small adjustments. For others, it will require a fundamental shift in how they think and how they sell.

That's why in this book we have presented the principles and big-picture skills as well as individual examples of D-gene-friendly actions. Some readers will learn by internalizing the principles, which will lead them to individual behaviors more or less automatically. Others, by trying out individual behaviors, will eventually come to adopt the underlying principles.

ON THE JOB

If you're serious about increasing your sales by expanding your base of women customers, there are several ways you can set up on-the-job learning experiences for yourself.

- ➤ Go back through the book, and identify a chapter that focuses on an area where you would like to improve. List two or three of the points in that chapter that strike you as especially important. Next to each point, identify a place where you could use that skill. Try it in a real situation. Evaluate how successful you were and decide what you need to do differently the next time.

- ➤ Find a colleague who has read the book. Choose a skill you'd each like to improve, and make a commitment to practice. After a few trial sales situations, get together and discuss what happened. Trade advice on what to do differently the next time.

➤ Set yourself a private goal of increasing your sales to women by a specific amount over the next six months. During this time keep track of how well you perform the skills in each of the five competencies, and where the greatest challenges are for you. If you meet your goal, take a few minutes to decide which skills made the difference. Then set a more challenging goal for the next six months.

ME? PRACTICE?

PLACE: United Center Arena in Chicago.
TIME: 6:20 PM.

At 8:05 the Chicago Bulls will be playing, but now there are fewer than a hundred fans in their seats.

On the court stands a six-foot, six-inch player wearing number 23. He is standing with his back to the basket, about thirteen feet out. Next to him is a rack of basketballs. He reaches for a ball, dribbles, launches himself into the air away from the basket, turns, and shoots while still in the air. He grabs another ball and does it again. And again. Jump, turn, shoot. Jump, turn, shoot.

The player is Michael Jordan, during his last week as an active player, and he is practicing his turnaround jumper. It is his signature shot. The other players? They're nowhere to be seen. They're taping their ankles, drinking soft drinks, talking to their agents, or reviewing their contracts.

Out there on the court, Number 23 continues to practice. It's been forty minutes now, and the stands are beginning to fill up, but his focus is absorbed by what he's doing. Jump, turn, shoot. Jump, turn, shoot.

If the world's best basketball player at the top of his power saw the need to practice his signature shot for forty minutes before a game, then who can say that hard work and practice are not necessary at every point in our careers, no matter how successful we are?

In this book we have provided the skills and principles you will need to achieve success selling cars and trucks to women. Making it happen is up to you. Like Michael Jordan, you have to want success enough to be willing to work hard. You have to keep practicing and learning. It worked for Michael Jordan. It can work for you.

FIRST THE MONEY, NOW THE GIRL

For Men Only

So far, we've concentrated on helping you get more money selling cars and trucks to women. Now it's time to help you get (or keep) the girl.

Can the skills in this book also help you improve your personal relationships with the opposite sex?

You can bet on it.

If you're like the men in our workshops, you've probably already been mentally trying out some of these concepts with your wife or girlfriend. So that's how she really thinks! No wonder she drives me crazy! No wonder I drive her crazy!

We'll never forget the participant in one of our seminars who came back late after the lunch break. "Sorry," he said, "I've been on the phone with my wife, apologizing for the last 15 years."

Understanding the D-gene does not mean you have to accept the blame for everything that happens in a relationship. Nor will it smooth out every rough patch you and your significant other experience. However, it sure can clear away a lot of futile arguments.

For Stan, a California stock broker, his first post-D-gene interaction had to do with a story his wife had wanted to tell him the night before. Here's the dialogue as he remembers it:

SHE: *Did you hear what happened to the Harners?*
HE: *No, what?*

SHE: *Well, I saw Marylou at the store today, and she seemed a little different. Some people can't hide their feelings, you know what I mean?*

HE: *Not exactly, but—*

SHE: *(interrupting) Well, with Marylou you can always tell how she's feeling just by looking at her.*

HE: *Uh huh. So what happened?*

SHE: *Well, you knew they'd been in couples therapy.*

HE: *No...*

SHE: *Yes, I told you last week!*

HE: *You did? OK, so... what happened?*

SHE: *Marylou said Doug has been expressing a lot of angry feelings in therapy, and she got frightened. Apparently Doug has a really dark side. I never thought of him in those terms, did you?*

HE: *You mean he hit her?*

SHE: *No . . .*

HE: *What happened, then?!*

SHE: *I'm trying to tell you!!*

HE: *Are they getting a divorce? Is that it?*

SHE: *No!*

HE: *(checking his watch) OK, look. I've got a lot of calls to return. Can we just cut to the chase here?*

"As soon as I heard myself say 'cut to the chase,' I realized we had a classic D-gene situation on our hands," he said. "I'm always telling her to 'cut to the chase,' and she *always* wants to give me the details. Now I realize it's just the damned D-gene."

Understanding alone won't automatically solve issues like this, but it makes them easier to deal with because it removes the element of blame. Stan's wife is not disorganized, nor is Stan cold-hearted. It's the D-gene. With any luck, once you understand the D-gene, you can stop wasting so much energy trying to change each other.

A WHOLE NEW LIGHT

There are many couples who would have very little to say if they stopped trying to change each other. Spousal Change, in fact, may be one of our most popular marital pastimes, especially early in a marriage, and it's one which women seem to approach with more fervor and a greater sense of purpose than men.

Think of a common "issue" between you and your wife or girlfriend. To what extent is it influenced by the D-gene? If you stopped trying to change her, what could you do about it?

Here's a list to get you started:

> *In an episode of the TV sitcom* Roseanne, *her sister is lamenting the fact that she can't find a man as good as Roseanne's husband.*
>
> *"You don't think he came out of the box this way, do you?" Roseanne retorts. "It took me years of hard work, and I'm still not finished."*

THE "ISSUE"	THE INFLUENCE OF THE D-GENE	WHAT YOU CAN DO
HE: *What's your point?!* **SHE:** *I'm trying to tell you. Stop rushing me!*	Context is important to a woman, while outcome is important to a man.	Sit back and relax. Don't look at your watch.
SHE: *You always interrupt me!* **HE:** *I do not!*	Although women's speech patterns allow interruptions, they don't like to be interrupted. To a man, interruptions are normal parts of any lively conversation.	Zip your lip. (This gets easier with practice.)

THE "ISSUE"	THE INFLUENCE OF THE D-GENE	WHAT YOU CAN DO
HE: *If he's not punished, he'll never learn.* **SHE**: *Everything is black or white to you!*	Women tend to consider personal circumstances when making judgments. Men tend to think in abstract, right-wrong terms.	Ask yourself how *you* would like to be judged, and be grateful that some members of the human race may be willing to show you some mercy.
SHE: *You're not listening!* **HE**: *I am, too!*	Women look for signs of active listening— nodding, smiling, commenting, while men tend to listen passively.	Respond. Nod. Say "uh huh."
SHE: *We need to talk.* **HE**: *Can we do it later? I'm trying to watch the game.*	Women derive more of their identity from relationships than men do.	Hit the "pause" button and give her your full attention. You can watch the game later. (This assumes you own that indispensable marital aid known as TiVo.)

SHARE THE KNOWLEDGE

One important difference to keep in mind is that your wife or girlfriend is not your customer. She is a full partner in your relationship. If you want to collaborate in a serious way with a special woman in your life, she will need to understand the D-gene, too. Give her the book, and ask her to read Chapter 3, "Decoding the D-gene," and Chapter 4, "Not Until She Trusts You."

We've found that when you have conflict, a little humor often helps. Here are some humorous men-made rules for women that we found circulating on the Internet.

> ➤ Sunday sports on TV are a force of nature, like the tides, or the phases of the moon. Don't get in the way.

➤ Ask directly for what you want. Hints do not work, even obvious hints. Just say it.

➤ If we ask what is wrong and you say "nothing," we will act like nothing's wrong. We know you think something's wrong, but we resent the energy required to tease it out of you.

➤ If you come to us with a problem, don't be surprised if we try to solve it for you. If it's only sympathy you want, make sure you tell us that. Otherwise, you might want to talk to your girlfriends.

➤ Christopher Columbus did not need directions and neither do we.

➤ I *am* in shape. Round is a shape.

After you've had a good laugh, have a good conversation. See what ideas she may have to deal with the D-gene. She may be eager to change a few of her own behaviors since she highly values your relationship.

GET CREATIVE

"The only time I have ever had a man pay attention to me—I mean, really pay attention, was when he was trying to get me into bed," Marsha said. "Not just the candy and flowers stuff, but listening and being attentive and remembering what I say. Of course, then you sleep with him and everything changes."

Marsha is not the first woman to make this observation. What's interesting here, however, is the parallel she suggests to the selling process. Once a prospect is wooed and won, do you take her for granted? Or, as one woman put it, "Is it only new customers who get special treatment and better rates?"

WORDS WOMEN USE (MEN TAKE HEED!)

FINE: *The word women use to end an argument when they are right and you need to shut up.*

FIVE MINUTES: *If she is getting dressed, half an hour; if you have just been given 5 more minutes to watch the game before doing a chore, this is 5 minutes.*

NOTHING: *"Something," and you should be on your toes. Arguments that begin with "Nothing" usually end with "Fine."*

GO AHEAD: *A dare, not permission. Don't do it.*

LOUD SIGH: *She thinks you are an idiot and wonders why she is wasting her time standing here and arguing with you over "Nothing."*

THAT'S OKAY: *She wants to think long and hard before deciding how and when you will pay for your mistake.*

THANKS: *Thanks. Just say you're welcome.*

If you take a look at the five principles of trust-based selling, you will see how directly they apply to a personal relationship:

➤ **T**hink relationship, not product.
➤ **R**espect her, her time, and her timing.
➤ **U**nderstand her on her own terms.
➤ **S**urpass her every expectation.
➤ **T**elegraph confidence.

Think about it… to sell effectively to a woman you need to do and say things to demonstrate that:

➤ You value your relationship with her above any sale.
➤ You have confidence and competence, yet you never manipulate or hurry her into a decision.
➤ You consider her a special individual with unique needs that cannot be satisfied with cookie-cutter solutions. She can expect special treatment from you.

> ➤ Because you listen carefully and remember what she tells you, you understand her situation, and offer help that is best for her in both the short and the long term.

> ➤ You know how to adapt yourself to her timing, along with her preferred style of communicating and decision making.

> ➤ Whenever you can, you will create solutions that will surprise and delight her, and give her stories about your creativity and thoughtfulness that she can regale her friends with.

If you show this list to your wife or girlfriend, we guarantee she'll say, "Hey, I'd like some of that!"

Also, trying out these ideas with your wife or girlfriend is a safe way to try out new approaches, fine-tune your new selling skills, and get the kind of honest feedback you could never get from a customer. In any event, once you begin to put the material in this book into practice at work, you will notice improvement in all your relationships with women—whether you make a conscious choice to apply it in your private life or not.

In the final analysis, everybody wins. You increase your sales. Your women customers form a relationship with a salesperson they trust to do right by them. And you can enjoy relationships with the important women in your life—wife, girlfriend, mother, daughter—free of those frictions and conflicts the D-gene can produce.

ABOUT MADDOX SMYE'S
HOW TO GET **RICH** SELLING TO WOMEN
SKILLS DEVELOPMENT PROGRAM

Maddox Smye LLC, was founded in 1993 with the mandate to help companies convert more women shoppers into buyers, long-term customers and vocal advocates. The stated mission is to "help leading edge companies close more sales by building enduring relationships with women."

Firm founder, Rebecca Maddox spent over 15 years researching and developing an understanding of what women value and how women think, shop, decide and buy. Collaborating together, Rebecca and co-founder, Marti Smye, Ph.D., renowned organizational behaviorist, used the research to pioneer a scientific approach to selling to women that consistently translates into incremental, measurable sales for a blue chip roster of client companies.

Maddox Smye's 12-week Skills Development Program is based on a one-of-a-kind, proprietary sales audit system that culminates in an individualized, confidential report on 63 criteria necessary to proficiently sell and serve women customers. With "real" data as the baseline, sales professionals attend a one-day workshop introducing the five core competencies required to become a woman's trusted advisor. The program continues with 11 additional weeks of coaching and clinics, using a wide range of technology and tools that aid participants in adapting behavioral skills and producing measurable results.

For more information on the *Maddox Smye How to Get RICH Selling to Women Skills Development System*, please visit our website at www.maddoxsmye.com.

ABOUT MADDOX SMYE'S

KEYNOTES AND PRESENTATIONS

A presentation or keynote address by Rebecca Maddox, MBA, CPA and founding principal of Maddox Smye is an effective way for your organization to gain valuable insights and information from the last 15 years of research and development that gave birth to the Maddox Smye *How To Get RICH Selling To Women* philosophy and methodology.

Rebecca Maddox has emerged as the definitive voice on gender-focused selling to women. She is a recognized member of the National Speakers Association and one of the most dynamic and entertaining keynote speakers you will hear. Rebecca speaks weekly, around the world, to audiences representing thirty-six different industries. A sampling of her keynote topics include:

How to Get RICH Selling to Women

In this interactive and energizing presentation, you will learn the five common sense principles that hold the key to building T.R.U.S.T. with women and the 5 core competencies required to close sales with women, the application of which has been reported to increase personal revenue by 45%.

To Women, You Are Not a Billion Dollar Corporation, You Are a Guy Named Dave!

Selling to women is a science, requiring both knowledge and action. Rebecca provides the knowledge—by introducing the 5-key competencies and the accompanying behaviors required to close sales to women. Your sales team provides the action—by implementing the strategies and tools from this presentation to experience immediate and significant results.

The New Frontier: From Competitive Advantage to Competitive Necessity

With women having responsibility for 89% of purchases today, if you still consider them a niche market you're already behind. Every year more sales are going to come from a purse and not a pocket in every consumer market. In this compelling presentation, Rebecca will help you position your sales force to get in the lead, close more sales to women and build the enduring relationships that result in loyalty and referrals.

For more information on Maddox Smye keynotes and presentations, please visit our website at www.maddoxsmye.com.

SHARE THE MESSAGE OF

HOW TO GET RICH SELLING CARS AND TRUCKS TO WOMEN!

WITH YOUR CLIENTS AND YOUR SALES TEAMS

To get information or order additional copies visit our website at: www.maddoxsmye.com

WRITE US AT:

300 5th Avenue South
Suite 101, Box 420
Naples, Florida 34102